THE FIGHT GOES ON

by

Robert Brown

Edited by
Joy Brown

All rights reserved
Blinded Veterans Association
Washington, DC

January 1994

Table of Contents

Dedication i

Foreword ii

Chapter I: Remembering 1

Chapter II: A Good Day at BVA 17

Chapter III: Signs Along the Way 32

Chapter IV: A Team for the Times 40

Chapter V: Families and Children 53

Chapter VI: Filling the Ranks 65

Chapter VII: Getting to Know Blind People .. 79

Chapter VIII: I'm Worried Doctor 92

Chapter IX: Standing with Us through
             the Years 107

Afterword 118

Dedication

This book is dedicated to the blinded veterans who shared their personal experiences and perspectives, and all who advised and guided us.

Yet, central in our thoughts are all the wonderful people who make up our BVA family, the friends of blinded veterans who stand with us as we carry on our fight, our battle for dignity and independence. You remembered what we had done and what we had lost. You cared though you never knew our names. Our book is dedicated to you.

Robert Brown

Foreword

The fight goes on . . . the battle against darkness still rages—the battle to defeat the prejudice and ignorance that have long made blindness an enduring tragedy.

In our first book, *Our Fight, A Battle Against Darkness,* we told the story of young soldiers returning home blind from the battlefields of World War II. They refused to accept the grim fate that life held in store for them as blind men and, together, they formed the Blinded Veterans Association. We chronicled the development of the organization they founded, their early efforts to find the help they needed, to obtain blind rehabilitation, and to take their rightful places in society. We told, too, of their determination to reach and help their fellow blinded veterans.

The Association they formed has endured nearly fifty years, and we have never wavered in our mission, our determination, to make a better life for America's blinded veterans. We have carried on the fight they began. It is the fight that begins anew whenever a veteran is blinded by shell fire, by a bullet, in a fiery plane crash, or by a cruel disease, and finds that he or she is now blind in a sighted world and must now fight for dignity and independence.

In this book, we want to tell how we are continuing this fight. We want to share the stories and experiences of blinded veterans and tell about the men and women

Foreword

of BVA and what they do. We want to tell of the exciting work of our blinded veteran volunteers and how the friends of BVA are doing so much to help in the fight.

And we want to tell you about blindness, what it is and what it is not, how it came to us, and may come to anyone. We know that blindness can be terrifying when it comes, no matter the cause, and that it may devastate the individual and the family. We want to tell how blinded veterans and their families are coping with blindness, and we want to share with you the things we have learned.

The years to come will be difficult and challenging for BVA. We would like to talk about some of the signs we see that tell us of new battles, new challenges ahead, as we try to help even more blinded veterans, and share with you our plans for meeting these challenges.

It is our hope that this book may help to achieve a greater appreciation of the service and sacrifice of America's blinded veterans, and a fuller understanding of the work of the Blinded Veterans Association . . . and why the fight goes on . . . why the fight must go on. We hope you enjoy our book.

Ronald L. Miller, Ph.D.
Executive Director
Blinded Veterans Association

Chapter I: Remembering

"I received orders to go to Vietnam in October 1967. I was a 2d lieutenant in the U.S. Marine Corps. I will never forget. It was on December 4, 1967, I was with my men clearing a mine field near DaNang. A mine exploded and I was badly hurt—my legs, my abdomen, my head. My right eye had to be removed immediately. I hoped that my left eye could be saved, and I kept hope alive for a long time. I had some sight in the eye for awhile. I remember it was like looking into a deep red spider web. But it finally had to be removed too. Now I have two plastic eyes."

Blinded veterans remember. There is always that day or that year, or that time when it happened—when a marine, soldier, seaman, or airman became a blinded veteran. Mental and physical wounds heal, and the pain and suffering may become part of the past. But being blinded or becoming blind is always remembered—remembered as a time of horror, panic and pain. Whether the veteran was blinded instantly, or after a long painful struggle was told he would never see again, it is the same and a time always remembered.

"I enlisted in the Marine Corps in February 1966 and I was discharged in July 1968. I dropped out of high school so I could join the Marines.

"I was trained as a mortar man and my unit was sent to Vietnam. I was with the 1st Marine Division

stationed in Quantri Province in Vietnam. I remember I had been in Vietnam only seven months. I was hurt on Christmas Day in 1967. We were unloading mortar and machine gun ammunition from a truck. I was carrying a case of machine gun ammunition and two mortar rounds, and one of the mortar rounds exploded.

"The blast blew out my right eye and filled my left eye with shrapnel, dislodging the retina from the optic nerve. The blast almost severed my left arm and shredded my left leg too.

"I regained consciousness in the hospital. I remember lying on a table and hearing a nurse screaming, 'Where do we start?' I remember saying, 'Any place will do.' "

Blinded veterans will often joke about the circumstances of their blinding. It seems to ease the pain and put a soft edge on the memory. But they remember, and the passing years seem to do little to help. Blinded veterans will often contact BVA on the anniversaries of their blinding. Being able to share the bad times with someone who understands, someone who has lived through the experience, does seem to help.

"I joined the U.S. Army in 1950 when the war in Korea was going on. I wanted to do my part for my country, and for me, a poor kid from California, the Army was a way to get ahead and away from the kind of life I was living. I knew I could get my education and a good job when I got out of the Army. I went to Korea as a rifleman with the 40th Infantry Division.

"It was July 11, 1952. We were out in front of our lines on a patrol trying to get into position to intercept enemy units moving up to the front. We got into a firefight

Chapter I: Remembering

and my unit came under close grenade attack. Grenades were landing right on us, and I was frantically throwing them back at the enemy. There was a terrible explosion. A grenade exploded in my hands before I could throw it back. My hands and face took the full force of the blast. Both of my hands were torn off and both of my eyes were burned and blasted away. A grenade blast is powerful and horrible.

"I remained conscious for a good while. I remember my buddies cutting off my boots and getting me onto a stretcher, and I remember being carried to the battalion aid station.

"The morphine I had been given took effect quickly and I wasn't in particularly great pain. But I knew I was in a very desperate situation, and I began to cry out that I wanted to die.

"I remember the Army doctor telling me, 'Corporal, you're too mean to die.' It seems that in my shock and horror I had been violently resisting his efforts to help me. I had to be tied down. They kept me alive though; they kept me from dying. That was long ago, and I've been doing okay. But I will always remember."

Remembering is important, as is the sharing of the memory. It's part of the grieving and healing process that may take a lifetime. When blinded veterans share these personal stories with those of us at BVA, they often fill them with humor and poke fun at themselves, but just as often, the stories are told in a matter-of-fact, somewhat resigned manner. Yet underneath the stories and their presentations, there are always the unspoken words, "I get so tired of being brave about this. I get so tired of telling people that I'm okay so they'll feel okay. Do people realize what I've lost and what I have to live with everyday?"

"In June 1966, I was with the 25th Division fighting in Vietnam. I was twenty-three and I had been in the Army over four years. I had planned on making the Army my career. My Infantry Company had been taking heavy machine gun and mortar fire, and we were preparing to advance into the area from which the fire was coming. We had to get through a mine field.

"My Company Commander sent me back to get a bulldozer to force a path through the mines. I brought the bulldozer up to the line and jumped off.

"I was standing there, discussing the coming attack with my Company Commander when there was a horrible explosion. The hydraulic system on the bulldozer had cut off and the heavy blade had dropped, jarring the ground and setting off an anti-tank mine close to where we were standing. The Company Commander and seven other men were killed.

"I never lost consciousness through everything that happened. I was blasted up into the air, and landed on my back. My left arm was shattered, my internal organs were mangled, my eyes were destroyed outright, and I was horribly burned too.

"A helicopter landed to take the wounded and dead men out. I was loaded aboard, and as we lifted off, the North Vietnamese were shooting at us, trying to shoot us down. I could hear the bullets hitting the helicopter. I didn't think we would make it. I remember trying to tell the medic that I was choking on my own blood, and I remember him clearing out my throat. And I remember the morphine taking hold and not feeling the pain anymore, just drifting off."

At BVA we sometimes argue whether it is better to

Chapter I: Remembering

lose one's sight all at once or to lose it over a period of time. It is often the totally blind guys, who lost their sight instantly, who will say that what happened to them, the manner in which they were blinded, quickly, was best. They will remark, "Once you're blind and there's no hope to regain your sight, then you can get about rebuilding your life; but if you lose your sight slowly, little by little, that keeps you in constant turmoil and depression, never knowing what's going to happen." Of course, there is no agreed upon answer to the debate. We would all agree, though, that sight is precious and if you can hang onto even a little bit of sight, it's a blessing.

"I was playing minor league baseball with a Chicago Cubs farm team. I got tired of it. I felt I was sitting on the bench too much, so I decided to try a career in the Marines. I joined up in January 1955. I got assigned to a Special Services unit attached to a Marine Air Wing based in El Toro, California.

"In 1962, when the situation in Vietnam began looking bad and they began sending in some U.S. military personnel, I was sent there as an instructor to help train the South Vietnamese Army. This was before the massive U.S. troop buildup in Vietnam. I was a staff sergeant at that time. During a hand-to-hand combat training exercise, I was struck in the head with the butt of an M1 rifle.

"I was knocked down, but I got up immediately. I didn't think too much of it. Things like that happened. I seemed to be okay. After awhile though, I noticed that I was having some problem seeing things at a distance and seeing things in front of me. Then I had some dizzy spells and nausea and seemed to be bothered by the

bright sunlight. I knew something was wrong with my eyes.

"When I got back to base, I went to a doctor, who at first thought I was just goofing off. But he examined me and then talked to another doctor, and then he remarked, 'You've got a problem.'

"I was sent back to Japan and then back to Camp Lejeune in North Carolina. After that, I was sent to Bethesda Naval Hospital near Washington, D.C., for six months while the doctors tried to figure out what had happened to me. Finally, the doctors told me I was going to be blind.

"They told me they thought the problem was severe macular degeneration, one of the worst cases they had seen. They also told me they thought I had something called rod and cone syndrome, a degeneration of the light receptors in the retina of the eye. It was a result of being struck in the head. There was nothing that could be done to save my eyesight."

At BVA, we remember, and we are reminded every day of the bitter harvest of war and the sacrifices of all veterans, particularly blinded veterans. We are also given daily reminders of the hideously destructive power of modern weapons of war, and that we send young men and women, young bodies, to confront this terrible power. We often shake our heads in amazement that human beings can survive such destruction. Blinded veterans remember these times of horror and death, of service and sacrifice, their long struggles to rebuild their lives, and pray that no more may suffer.

"I was an Army sergeant. I was twenty-four years old at the time. I was serving with the 1st Air Cavalry Division in Vietnam. I had ten days to go before I could

Chapter I: Remembering

go home.

"We were in the field, clearing out old land mines originally placed there by the French when they were fighting in Vietnam. It was an extremely dangerous job. One of the old mines blew up when it was touched, and in an instant it was over for me. I was blasted into the air. I vividly remember thinking as I was in the air, 'Well, you've just been killed.'

"I realized when I landed on the ground that I was still alive. I decided right then to fight to stay alive. But it was to be a hard fight. I was in bad shape. Among other things, both of my arms were broken, part of my liver had been sliced away, and my jugular vein was cut. I had five major wounds any one of which could have been fatal. I recovered from my wounds, but I will never see anything again."

* * * * * * * * * * * *

"I was just over eighteen years old when I was drafted. I was a private, a rifleman, in the U.S. Army when I was wounded on a hill in Korea in 1952. An artillery shell hit our position. It happened so quickly. I remember lying on the ground, stunned, trying to speak while my buddies tried to put pressure bandages on my wounds. That's all I can remember. Twenty-one days later, I came to in the Army hospital in Tokyo.

"When I woke up, one of my arms and one leg was in traction and my head was heavily bandaged. I remember the Army nurse who was sitting at my bedside. She told me that I was going to pull through but that I was blind—they had to remove my eyes. I remember that the bad news didn't really surprise me *that much. Thinking back, somehow I knew at that moment when I was hit that I would never see again."*

* * * * * * * * * * * *

"I was blinded, totally and instantly, in Vietnam when I was in the Marine Corps. I dropped out of school in the tenth grade and worked for awhile and then joined the Marines in November 1967 at the height of the war. I soon found myself with the 1st Marines, fighting in the Quon Long area of Vietnam.

"I remember, it was September 29, 1968. I was on patrol. It was a Viet Cong booby trap that got us. The device was a large charge of plastic explosive rigged up to go off at the slightest movement. I knew I was blind immediately. I got the full blast right in my face. It burned my face and eyes. I believe that the Marine who tripped the booby trap was killed, but I never knew for sure."

Women constitute a growing number of the blinded veterans BVA tries to help. In recent years, more and more women have taken their places in the military services which, while not specifically combat assignments, often place them at great risk. They are truly veterans, faithful, highly trained and highly motivated young Americans who went where they were told to go, and did what they were told to do. They also remember, and the stories of how they lost their sight are no less tragic or traumatic.

"I came from a military family. My father was in the U.S. Air Force for many years, so it was no surprise when I joined the Air Force too. To me it was the logical thing to do even though I am a woman.

Chapter I: Remembering

"I enlisted in March 1976 and I was trained as a telecommunications specialist. Eventually, I was assigned to the 1st Combat Communications Squadron in Weisbaden, Germany. We had to be ready to pack up everything at a moment's notice and be able to move to any crisis spot in Asia, Europe, or the Middle East and set up air-ground combat communications. As I recall, there were only five other women in my unit. We trained all the time.

"In 1978, my unit was sent to Pakistan for joint exercises. I had to take some shots and pills to protect against a deadly strain of malaria that could be picked up in Pakistan. I was sick the entire time I was in Pakistan. I lost ten pounds but I stayed on the job.

"One day my superior officer noticed I was looking more closely at the keyboard and monitor and he asked me if there was anything wrong with my eyes. I thought it might have to do with my being sick. It didn't get better, so I had my eyes checked when my unit returned to Germany. The doctors told me that I had some vision loss, though not enough to worry about.

"But my eyes kept getting worse and I finally found out what was happening. It was the medications I had taken before going to Pakistan. The odds were 1 in 10,000 that the medications could cause blindness. The odds were against me, though; I was that one."

As with the veteran above, blindness came to many of the veterans we work with in slow, inexorable, terrorizing increments. For these veterans, too, there will always be the day, the time, when they passed from the sighted world to the world of the blind.

"I am blind now. I was a Marine in Vietnam. I was one of those who made it through okay. I lost my sight

later. I'll tell you how it happened.

"I joined the U.S. Marine Corps on June 5, 1967 and went to boot camp at San Diego, California. They trained me as an artilleryman and then I was sent to Vietnam. I remember it was just before Thanksgiving in 1967. The memories of my time in Vietnam are still with me. I flew to war on a jet plane.

"It was pitch dark when we landed and, frankly, I was somewhat frightened about where I was and what lay ahead for me. I was assigned to a 105-howitzer unit, told to get onto one of the trucks in a convoy, and I was on my way to Phubai. A month later, we were sent to Hwei, and after that we were loaded aboard a ship and sent to the Philippines for refitting. Then we were sent back to Hwei.

"In April 1968, my unit was helicoptered, howitzers and all, to the mouth of the Qua Viet River. We fired a lot of artillery support for the Marine infantry, and we had a lot of casualties from incoming fire from North Vietnamese guns that had greater range and firepower than our guns. I can recall the planes spraying Agent Orange on the nearby jungle, trying to defoliate the trees so we could spot enemy movements.

"Then my unit was sent to the top of a mountain near the DMZ where we provided artillery support for the Marines at Kaeson. I still recall our furious fight to keep the North Vietnamese from overrunning the base. Then my time in Vietnam was up, and I was still alive and unhurt. I headed for home in December 1968 on a jet plane.

"I was discharged from the Marines and I returned home to Chicago. I went back to school, and then got a job in data processing. I got married, too.

Chapter I: Remembering

"One morning, it was in May 1973, I woke up and found that my thumb on my left hand was numb. After a few days of this, I went to a doctor who sent me to a neurologist. I was given a lumbar puncture, a spinal tap, and was informed that I had multiple sclerosis, or MS as it is usually called.

"I still felt fine and, for a time, took the whole matter very lightly. However, by 1978, I was in really serious trouble. Everything became blurry and my sight started to fade away. Then I started having other problems with my legs and then my internal organs. Now I can no longer walk and must use a wheelchair. I am also blind now."

Remembering is more than just recalling the time of loss, that time of pain and panic. It's also telling of the fight to recover—finding rehabilitation, learning to hope, and taking the first steps in a new life. In part, it's looking back, not in anger, but reliving old experiences with new perspectives and acceptance and often humor at what life has brought. Remembering reinforces determination to go forward and is part of the celebration of achievements made in a new life.

"My name is Gerard Boucher. I live in Haverhill, Massachusetts. I've lived here most of my life. It's a small town not far from Boston. I went to vocational school here and I joined the Marines here after I graduated. It was in 1966, and the war was going on in Vietnam. I was notified that I was going to be drafted into the Army.

"That didn't appeal to me, so I went and talked to the Navy recruiter. I had already received a lot of machine shop training while I was in vocational school and I thought I could get trained to be a machinist in

the Navy. My plans were to eventually get to be a tool and die maker. The Navy would have sent me to machinist school, but I got to thinking about it, and decided I wouldn't like being aboard a ship. I didn't like the water that much.

"Then I talked to the Marine Corps recruiter who told me if I joined the Marines I could hold off going in for a few months, and then I would be sent to machinist school when I finished boot camp. I thought that would be okay. I thought the war in Vietnam was sure to be over by that time and I wouldn't have to be in it. I joined the Marines in September 1966.

"I was sent to Parris Island for boot camp. Then I was trained as a machine gunner, given some special jungle training and sent to Vietnam. It was now June 1967 and I was nineteen years old.

"So there I was in Vietnam with the 1st Marines. I remember it was the rainy season, the monsoon season, and it rained continuously, and we were fighting continuously. I was a member of a machine gun team.

"One day we were ordered to try to interdict Viet Cong units carrying rice from the villages to their underground bunkers in the hills. Our orders were to set up a night ambush at a point the Viet Cong would have to approach as they moved toward the village. We were told that it would be dark and rainy and it would be hard for the Viet Cong to see us. But that night it wasn't raining or even overcast. That night the skies were clear and the moon was bright. It lighted up our ambush position like a spotlight. Our position was exposed, and we were sitting ducks, but orders were orders.

"The Viet Cong fired a mortar round that landed

Chapter I: Remembering

directly in front of our machine gun position. One of the guys was killed outright. He was standing watch a little to one side. I was due to relieve him in a few minutes. The other member of our team was wounded; I heard later he was badly hurt.

"The mortar round went off in front of me, into my face, and filled my head and face and eyes full of burning hot shrapnel. The blast knocked me down onto the ground, but I got back on my feet and put my hands to my head. It was all dirt and blood. I knew I had been badly hurt and I went into a rage. I couldn't see, but I tried to reach the machine gun. I just wanted to blast away at them for what they had done to us.

"Our machine gun position was at the bottom of a hill near the stone wall of an old cemetery. My buddies grabbed me and dragged me back behind the stone wall. I was in such awful pain from the burning metal in my head that I was screaming for God to take me.

"That's all I remember about that day. When I came to I was in the Army hospital in DaNang and I remember asking the doctor if I had any brain damage. He said, 'Obviously not, since you are asking about it.' But I wasn't told anything about my eyes.

"Then I was airlifted to Clark Air Force Base in the Philippines and then flown back to the States. My head was all bandaged and no one would give me a straight answer about my eyes. Then one day at the Naval Hospital in Massachusetts, my regular doctor was out, and another doctor was making the rounds. I asked him about my eyes. He told me I would never be able to see anymore. That's another day I will always remember.

"But I was able to hang onto a little bit of sight.

It's not much. My left eye is gone. My right eye can detect light and movement. I can't use it for anything, but it's some sight at least. After I recovered from my wounds, I went to the VA Blind Rehabilitation Center at Hines, Illinois. I enjoyed it, and it helped me tremendously.

"Over the years I have tried to work and continue my education. I never did become a tool and die maker. I received my AA degree in 1973, and for awhile worked for a company that manufactures reading machines for the blind and disabled.

"I remember how it was when I finally got back on my feet and went to college. I was a blinded Marine and the war in Vietnam was still going on. So much for getting training as a machinist. That was okay though. But there was a lot of emotion and protest going on against the war and a lot of it was directed toward me. That was hard to take. I recall one college professor telling me that we had no reason to be there in Vietnam, the war was a waste of time. It really made me feel bad. I told him the United States was there to advance freedom and democracy, and that I believed that if you went into the military service you should do your job. Our servicemen were representing our country whether the war was right or wrong. I asked him, 'Would you let someone kill your brother, or would you try to defend him? If you cared for your country you would fight for it.' That's how I feel and that's how veterans feel.

"My experiences as a blinded veteran have made me extremely concerned and supportive of all veterans. I try to do everything I can to help all veterans and work as best I can on their behalf. The veterans were out

there alone, doing their best to help their country, and they need help from us now. I became active with veterans issues almost immediately after I was well enough to get around. There are a lot of reasons, but mainly because of my friend who was killed at the time I was hurt. I owed him that.

"*I guess being blind is something you sort of get used to, although not really. I try to find the funny part of it, and laugh at myself. I've had some interesting experiences as a blind person. For example, I use a white cane in getting around and I hold it in front of me in my own way, in order to use the cane along with the little sight I have, and get the best out of both my eye and my cane. Once I was crossing a busy street and a car ran over my cane. You can guess how I reacted. I was mad. I went down to the machine shop where I used to work and showed the guys what had happened to my cane. I told them I wanted a cane made out of solid steel. They made me one, but it weighed five and a half pounds. However, no car can break it. (I use it now as a chin-up bar.)*

"*There are a lot of problems blinded veterans have to cope with. Reading is always a big problem for the blind. We can get things on tape or in braille, and there are some pretty good reading machines too, but it's best when another person can read for you. Mostly it's finding someone who can fit into your schedule and be there to read when you need help. A really successful blind person will have a pool of readers to draw upon. I'm back in school now and it's a big issue for me.*

"*I learned braille as soon as I could, although I'm not using braille that much now. Back when I was first blinded, I wanted to learn to read braille really fast, so I could get to the real juicy part of a book. But it was too slow getting to the good part I wanted to read. I do make good use of a battery powered device called a Braille and Speak. A lot of blinded veterans can still use a CCTV, a closed circuit TV system for reading. However, even with this level of magnification, it's a wicked strain for blind people who have to work with a CCTV. I can no longer use one.*

"You can see by my story that life does go on, and I'm learning to cope with blindness. All blinded veterans get on with life sooner or later. The Blinded Veterans Association and other blinded veterans are a big part of this process. I enjoyed sharing my memories with you."

Remembering, telling, sharing, they are all part of the process of healing and coping. We would tell our readers that all of the blinded veterans whose memories we have shared have been helped by BVA and are moving ahead and doing well. In sharing their stories, we hope that you may remember what they did and what they sacrificed for all of us.

Chapter II: A Good Day at BVA

I want to tell you about our Association—the Blinded Veterans Association—and about those of us who work here, and why we feel the work we do is so vitally important. I want you to get to know the men and women who work at our BVA National Headquarters in Washington, D.C. and at BVA stations in the field. I want to tell you about the work we do, and most of all, I want to give you a sense of the spirit that keeps us on the job, helping America's blinded veterans.

Let me begin by telling you that at the end of the workday we are all quite tired, and that is all I will say about how hard we work. It's the work we do and the Association we operate that I most want to tell you about.

An interesting phenomena occurs each night when we close the office, set the special locks on the door, and put the telephones on the night line. It's when we say good night to each other and leave to go home.

I often watch from my office near the front door of our building as the staff leaves for the evening, and I still have enough sight and hear enough to know, by the way they walk, by the way they say good night, by the way they linger a few moments and exchange a joke or share some parting remarks, or talk of work which must be done tomorrow; I can tell if it's been a good day at BVA.

The Blinded Veterans Association is an unusual organization. We are a congressionally chartered veterans service organization. We received our charter from the U.S. Congress in 1958, and our organization is officially recognized by public law as being responsible for helping blinded veterans. While BVA is a veterans service organization, it is much more. BVA is many things, and I want to tell you about the various parts of our organization and what it takes to operate our Association.

BVA was organized in 1945 by a small group of veterans who returned home blind from the battlefields of Europe. They didn't like and wouldn't accept what life held in store for them as blind individuals, so they set about the task of making the world a better place for all blind people. They were veterans and they formed an association of veterans—the Blinded Veterans Association—with the goal of providing mutual aid and assistance to one another. They organized to be able to help one another so that they would not have to face the world blind and alone.

Our mission is to reach out to blind and visually impaired veterans and their families and provide whatever assistance we can: counseling, support services, benefits information, job development and placement, and representation when a blinded veteran needs help in pursuing a claim before the Department of Veterans Affairs. But our mission is more than this.

Much of our work involves trying to bring official and public attention to the needs of blinded veterans, indeed, all veterans and all blind people. This means we must work with committees of the U.S. Senate and the U.S. House of Representatives, and federal agencies

Chapter II: A Good Day At BVA

such as the Department of Veterans Affairs, and do our best to advance and advocate legislation and programs that will help blinded veterans.

We are a membership organization, too. We would like all blinded veterans to join BVA and, to this end, BVA keeps membership rates at a very low, nominal level so every blinded veteran may become a BVA member regardless of economic circumstances. We never require membership for our services. In fact, when we talk to a blinded veteran, we rarely ask if he or she is a BVA member. I am happy that this has always been our policy. It makes it a lot easier when we are working with a veteran who is going blind and is distraught and depressed, and who just needs help.

A good part of our daily work centers around services to our members. There is a lot to it. BVA is run by the membership assembled and voting in convention. Our National Officers and District Directors are elected by the membership. Our affiliate groups, we call them our BVA Regional Groups, are run by BVA members. Our members are very active and interested in BVA affairs, and many of them are on the phone with us frequently. And it's a big job keeping membership rolls accurate and up-to-date.

Communicating with blinded veterans is always problematic. How does one do it effectively? They don't read, or can't read as other people do. We have learned through long experience that it takes an extra effort to communicate with distant members. For many of our blinded veterans, trying to read is just too exhausting, and unless a spouse or family member will do the reading for them, they will just do without. Happily, BVA has found the way to do it. Since 1946, we have never failed to send out the scheduled issue of the *BVA BULLETIN*. Blinded veterans look forward to receiving it and we hear immediately if someone hasn't received their *BVA BULLETIN*.

We send the *BVA BULLETIN* to nearly twenty thousand blinded veterans six times a year. It's sent out in both large print and tape cassette format. The *BVA BULLETIN* is our primary means of communicating with blinded veterans and the public, and we try to send out as much useful information as possible. Preparing the *BVA BULLETIN* is a big job too, but it's certainly worth it.

I mentioned that our organization is controlled by the membership meeting in convention. We hold an annual convention, usually outside of Washington, D.C. Our BVA conventions are sponsored by a previously selected Regional Group, but the work of planning and carrying out the convention falls on the staff at our National Headquarters. Some of our readers may have had the opportunity to do convention or meeting planning, and may know the incredible amount of detailed coordination and arrangements that have to be worked out. And no sooner do we finish one convention than we have to start on the next.

BVA also operates as a charitable organization. We were established as a not-for-profit corporation and we are registered with the Internal Revenue Service as a 501(C)(3) charitable organization. This means that BVA can legally conduct fund raising activities and accept charitable contributions. Donors may include their contributions to BVA as charitable deductions in their own tax accounting as authorized by federal and state laws.

Chapter II: A Good Day At BVA

This aspect of BVA is extremely important. All of the funds that we use to operate the Association and carry out our programs come to us through charitable contributions. We get no support from the federal or state governments. There is a lot of work that goes into raising money for BVA. It's work that never stops. BVA sends out seven direct mail fund raising appeals each year. Perhaps one of the less pleasant parts of our work is asking for money, but it has to be done. It is really great that we're able to keep BVA going through the generous support of so many caring Americans.

We seem to have an inordinate amount of administrative work for such a small organization. There is a tremendous amount of detail in running veterans service programs, affiliate groups, membership, raising funds, and just administering BVA. We often remark, "How can such a small organization have so much paperwork?"

Working at BVA is certainly challenging, and keeping BVA going takes a lot of effort, but all of us look on our work as our mission. It's more than just a job. There is a special feeling that comes over everyone who works at BVA for awhile. For sure, we do get paid for our work, but we believe we are doing good things, helping people who need help, and it's great to have the chance to do this.

Of course, we do, upon occasion, gripe and complain some. I know I do, especially when I'm tired or when I've been unsuccessful in trying to help a blinded veteran. There are days when nothing seems to click and we can't get on top of our work. But most days are good days at BVA.

I work with some really great people. They are skilled

and talented in doing their jobs. Some of them are real characters, too, and I suppose they might say the same about me. I am proud to call them all my friends.

Ron Miller is our Executive Director. His office is on the third floor of the small building that serves as BVA's National Headquarters. Let me digress a moment and tell you about our building.

BVA moved into the building in July 1988. This is the first time we have had our own National Headquarters building. Our members set up a special building fund and saved for many years to get the money to make the down payment on our own BVA building. As I mentioned, it's small, but there is space enough for now and for the future. We are very proud of it, and I hope our readers will get the chance to stop in and visit us if they get a chance to come to Washington, D.C.

BVA is located in the Chinatown section of the city. We are about equidistant from the White House and Capitol Hill, and close to the Department of Veterans Affairs. We're also close to the subway and a lot of good Chinese restaurants.

It's an old building, erected in the 1870s and listed as a historical site. Over the years, the building has served many purposes: as a school, a church, a mission, community center, and bank. It's sort of a spooky place at night, though. Sometimes when I'm alone and working late in the evening, the creaking and groaning of the old timbers and the rustling of the window shades can make me jumpy. And there's that old story that long ago some tragedy occurred in the building and that a spirit may be afoot. I really wouldn't know about that. Washington, D.C. is full of such stories.

Chapter II: A Good Day At BVA

Now, back to Ron Miller. He's Ronald L. Miller, Ph.D. He's been BVA's Executive Director since 1985. Ron is totally blind; he lost his sight while in the Marines. Ron has a doctorate in history and had been a college professor. He was the State Director for Veterans Employment and Training in California before coming to BVA. Ron has served in various BVA National Officer positions too, and served two terms as BVA's National President. I look at Ron as our office intellectual. Ron has the amazing capacity to immediately assess the central issue of any problem taken to him. I often go to his office ready to brief him on what I feel is a complex issue only to find he is way ahead of me in thinking it through. Ron sets the mood for the office and gets us working as a team.

Much of the BVA Executive Director's time is spent on administrative and management matters, as well as working with our National Officers, our District Directors, and officials of BVA affiliate groups. The primary responsibility for convention planning falls on Ron, too. Ron uses a dog guide, a German shepherd. "Hunter" is a friend and favorite of all of us. Hunter is part of the team, always happy to see us, and to greet us with his cold, wet nose.

Another member of our staff is named Miller. Tom Miller is the Director of Governmental Relations and responsible for BVA's legislative and governmental affairs. It's Tom's job to prepare our BVA legislative program, coordinate with other veterans service organizations such as the Veterans of Foreign Wars, the Disabled American Veterans and the Paralyzed Veterans of America, and to testify before Congress on matters affecting blinded veterans. He also works closely with the Department of Veterans Affairs and other federal agencies in developing and strengthening programs for blinded veterans.

Tom is totally blind, too. He was blinded in Vietnam while serving with the U.S. Marines. I also think Tom is amazing. I've watched him testify before Congress and speak for blinded veterans at government meetings. He is a real professional and highly respected by his colleagues in other organizations. He likes to argue an issue and I think he would have made a good lawyer. Tom has also served as BVA National President, and joined the BVA National Headquarters staff in 1986.

I have talked about the mass of administrative work our small Association has to do. John Williams is our Administrative Director and has been with BVA since 1990. John had a long career as an officer in the U.S. Marine Corps. He is sighted and, consequently, we have placed a great deal of the paperwork load and administrative work on him, everything from getting the roof repaired to overseeing activities of BVA Regional Groups. John does it all, and more. And at our conventions and meetings of our Board of Directors, John is often the only one there who can see. So John has to manage the proceedings and do all the reading.

Jun Uy is the Comptroller and Financial Manager. Jun is sighted. He is a native of the Philippines, and has been with BVA since 1990. As much as anyone, Jun is responsible for the improved level of financial stability BVA now enjoys. He has made some really positive changes in how we budget and spend our scarce resources; he makes every dollar count. Jun has dramatically reduced our administrative and management overhead costs, too, and made it possible to use more of our resources in helping blinded veterans. Thanks, Jun.

Jun is serious about his job and his work, but he is also our office comic. At the end of the day, when he closes the ledgers and turns off the accounting computer, when we are all feeling a little run over, we can count on Jun to get us laughing at ourselves.

I spoke of BVA as being a charitable organization. Cheryl Swaim is our staff member responsible for this part of BVA operations. Cheryl is our Director of Development. That means she is our fund raiser. We depend on Cheryl's energy and commitment, and we depend on Cheryl for the funds it takes to keep BVA operating.

Cheryl raises money for BVA by sending out seven direct mail appeals each year. It's a difficult way to raise money and it is not an inexpensive way, either. It's difficult in that BVA has to compete with a multitude of other organizations, most of them very worthy organizations, to raise enough money to keep going. It's expensive in that costs for postage, envelopes, paper, printing, and everything associated with a direct mail fund raising program go up continually. Unfortunately, there is no other way to do it. There's probably more pressure on Cheryl than anyone on the staff, and we all try to do our part to help. Cheryl joined BVA in 1992, after years of experience as BVA Account Executive with a firm that advises us on fund raising. Cheryl is a real professional in a tough business.

I talked previously about our *BVA BULLETIN*. Chris Bentley, our Communication Coordinator, is responsible for preparing and editing the *BVA BULLETIN* and making sure blinded veterans receive it. It's our major publication and in the two years Chris has been with BVA, he has greatly improved the quality and quantity of information we send out. Chris has an excellent speaking voice, and does the voice taping for the *BVA BULLETIN* and other releases. Actually, he sounds just like a professional radio announcer. Chris is in charge of all of BVA's dealings with the media such as radio, TV, and the press. He has done a good job in telling the public who we are. Chris is a sighted veteran who spent several years in the U.S. Army before coming to BVA.

Alyson Alt is our Membership Manager and has been with BVA nearly seven years. Alyson spends much of her day on the telephone or at her computer terminal, talking and working with members and resolving membership problems. When our members have a question of almost any nature, Alyson is the one they call because she's the one they know. Alyson has done a superb job for BVA in getting more blinded veterans to sign up as members. Increasing membership is a constant struggle. Many of our World War II blinded veterans are now passing away. It's Alyson's job to deal with this sad fact too, and she still keeps membership growing.

I'm the National Field Service Director, and my name is Robert Brown. I still have a little sight left in one eye. I was in the Army for three years back during the Korean war. The Marines here on the staff—Ron, Tom, and John—sometimes make pointed remarks about my having been in the Army. I've learned to put up with it.

I lost my sight after leaving military service and had good sight until about fifteen years ago. I've been with BVA since 1985. Ron and Tom are totally blind and use computers with voice synthesizers. My vision is still good enough for me to read with a closed circuit TV system and I use a computer with a large print display.

The BVA Field Service Program extends our services directly to blinded veterans and their families. I supervise a staff of six Field Service Representatives stationed throughout the country. They are all highly skilled, highly motivated blinded veterans. I will tell you about them shortly, but first, I want to introduce you to our support staff at the National Headquarters who help us do our work and are responsible in great part for keeping BVA running smoothly.

Rosemary Butcher is Ron Miller's Executive Assistant and also does much of the work in planning and managing BVA conventions. To us, Rosemary is superwoman, always ready and able to deal with any problem. Most of all, I think of Rosemary as one who is truly concerned about BVA and blinded veterans and cares about her co-workers.

Michelle Gailes is Tom Miller's Secretary, reader and all-round assistant. Michelle came to BVA only recently. She has the unique distinction of being the only woman veteran on the staff, having served four years in the Army.

Yvonne Preston is our Bookkeeper and works with Jun Uy. Yvonne has been with us about seven years, and she is one of the busiest persons at BVA. She is the one who is always remarking about how such a small organization can have so much paperwork. She handles accounts receivable, accounts payable, payroll, travel expenses, bank deposits, you name it, Yvonne is responsible for it. And Yvonne is never too busy to drop what she's doing and take care of you.

Shonda Northam works with Cheryl Swaim, handling the myriad details involved in running the direct mail program. In an average year, we send out several million pieces of mail, and receive thousands of returns. It all has to be processed and that's what Shonda works on.

Brigette Jones is BVA's Administrative Assistant and works closely with John Williams. Brigette has been with BVA about four years. She's also one of those people who is able to handle any problem and is a great asset to BVA.

Vira Hong is my secretary and reader and Administrative Assistant for the Field Service Program. Vira is a native of Cambodia and has traveled and studied throughout the world, accompanying her father who was a diplomat. She has been with BVA longer than any of us, nearly fifteen years. Vira is my right hand. I cannot count the number of times she has reminded me of things I needed to do, or corrected me when I was about to make the wrong decision. Vira has much to do with my having a good day at BVA.

And Crystal Sturdivant recently joined our staff as BVA's Receptionist. Crystal has one of the most important jobs at BVA. Her voice is the first voice a blinded veteran hears when calling BVA, and it's a caring, helpful voice. Crystal also helps with data entry and helps me too, since my office is near the reception desk.

As you can see, I'm proud of the men and women

Chapter II: A Good Day At BVA

who work at BVA National Headquarters. Now, I want to tell you about our staff in the field, our BVA Field Service Representatives—our "Field Reps." They are BVA's front line troops; they are blinded veterans, and they work one-on-one with blinded veterans.

George Brummell was a sergeant in the U.S. Army. He was blinded, totally, in the Vietnam War. George is stationed at the VA Regional Office in Washington, D.C. He is an excellent role model for newly blinded veterans. When a newly blinded veteran and family members see what George can do, the effect is dramatic. I've seen it myself. George and I recently visited a newly blinded veteran at Walter Reed Army Hospital. The veteran had been shot in the head and totally blinded. His mother and father were in the room when we visited him. They had talked to us previously and saw little hope of a life for their son as a blind person. George Brummell showed what he could do as a blind man. We were in the room for less than an hour. I remember the veteran's father and mother starting to relax and smile. George is on the road much of the time, meeting blinded veterans and showing them they can go on with life, too.

Larry Grant is BVA's Field Rep in Boston. Larry served for years in the U.S. Air Force Strategic Air Command, and was a company manager before becoming legally blind and coming to work for BVA. Larry is our newest Field Rep, but his management talents have already been amply demonstrated. He has pushed ahead quickly in setting up volunteer activities and strengthening our Regional Groups in the New England States. Larry has made it a point to call all the blinded veterans in his area on their birthdays, if he hasn't heard from them in a while. Larry doesn't wait for problems to develop.

Norman Jones is our Field Rep in Atlanta. Norman was a paratrooper with the U.S. Army's 82d Airborne Division. He lost his sight, totally, due to glaucoma after he left the service. Like George and Larry, Norman is on the road much of the time. Norman has a special sensitivity, a quiet, unassuming style that works well with blinded veterans who are frightened and upset. He's a great asset to BVA.

Arthur Mathews is our Field Rep in Chicago. Arthur was in the Marines, and was blinded in Vietnam. He has a little sight remaining in one eye, but very little. Art is the champion of lost causes, and will fight to the last to help a blinded veteran get the help he or she needs. And much of the time, his hard work pays off. Like the other Field Reps, Art travels throughout his assigned states, helping his fellow blinded veterans, setting up volunteer programs and working with BVA Regional Groups.

Peter Link is our Field Rep stationed in Denver. Peter served in the U.S. Air Force and lost his sight to retinitis pigmentosa. He is essentially totally blind. Peter is my expert on VA rules and regulations that apply to blinded veterans claims. The more complex the issue, the more Peter likes to dive in and solve it. Peter too, travels much of the time, working with blinded vets in the midwestern states.

Larry Martinez is our Field Rep for the West Coast and my Assistant Field Service Director. I rarely see him because he's stationed in Sacramento, California. However, we talk on the telephone several times a day. Larry was a sergeant in the U.S. Air Force and is legally blind from macular degeneration. Larry is BVA's expert in finding jobs and job training for blinded veterans. Many, many blinded veterans now holding down good jobs can thank Larry Martinez.

I guess you can see how very proud I am of our Field Reps. They are all blind and all travel and work independently. Last year, this small group of blind men worked one-on-one with over two thousand newly blinded veterans. I wish our readers could spend just one day with them as they go about their work. I wish our readers could spend just one day with those of us who work at BVA Headquarters and watch as we carry out the mission entrusted to us. I think you would say you had a good day at BVA.

Chapter III: Signs Along the Way

"Tell us, friend, what is the road that stretches before us? Will you read the signs, for we are blind and cannot see."

"My dear sirs, there are many signs and many roads. You are at a crossroad. So tell me, where does your journey take you?"

"We journey from the past into a new time. The old way is behind us. We must travel a new road. So read if you will, all the signs, that we may know and choose the road ahead."

In many ways, the Blinded Veterans Association is at a crossroad. We see the signs, but they are not easy to read. It would be great if all the signs were clear, or there was someone to tell us precisely what the signs indicate and which road we should take. There are different roads that BVA could choose to travel. And, all the signs, all the roads, mean challenge and change. Some of the signs clearly tell us what lies ahead and leave little doubt about the future, others are not so easily read, and understanding the signs, choosing the right road, and guiding our Association will, indeed, be the challenge.

Assessing the future is a difficult task, and accurate forecasting is usually impossible. Yet, even in our own lives there are signs which, if simply read and heeded, would keep us on the right path. Sadly, as we travel

Chapter III: Signs Along the Way

the road of life, we often read too late or missed the signs, especially the detour signs that would have led to the right road.

What lies ahead for the Blinded Veterans Association and America's blinded veterans? Some of the signs, the answers, are clear but many are hard to read. As friends of BVA sharing our concerns for the future, we would share with you, too, some of the signs that we see. Call them signs or call them challenges, they will essentially determine the course of the Blinded Veterans Association in years to come.

One of the signs foremost in our thoughts these days is that BVA will soon be fifty years old. We are proud of the fact—fifty years of continuing work and efforts on behalf of America's blinded veterans. What a difference BVA has made in the lives of all blinded veterans. We have accomplished much, and that, in a way, is what concerns us. There is so much left to do, and the gains we have made can so easily slip away or be taken away.

We must remember the bold dream of the young men returning home blind from the battlefields of Europe and the Pacific, and ensure that BVA remains true to that dream and that the dream endures. And now, in the last decade of the twentieth century, we wonder what events, what changes, in the decades ahead will mean for BVA and the blinded veterans who will seek our help.

America's veterans are getting older too. Right now, there are nearly 29 million veterans. During World War II alone, the United States had over 16 million men and women under arms. Think of it, if a soldier was age nineteen when he was drafted in 1943, he would be sixty-nine years old today. And if a man was nineteen in 1950 when he was drafted to fight in Korea, he would be sixty-two today. The same is true with the veterans of the Vietnam War and the long, long years of the cold war. Time, as it will, marches on. The implications and signs for change are many. Maintaining and expanding health care programs for our aging veteran population is an urgent issue for BVA as well as for all veterans service organizations. Maintaining and expanding services for an increasing number of older veterans with vision problems is a particularly worrisome challenge for BVA.

The numbers of blinded veterans will increase dramatically in the coming years. According to figures developed by the American Foundation for the Blind, and based on the percentage of blind persons in the population not counting the congenitally blind and blind adolescents, there may be as many as 120,000 blinded veterans today. This includes veterans blinded in military service and those who have lost their sight through illness, disease and injury.

A study prepared in August 1991 by Gregory L. Goodrich, Ph.D. for the Department of Veterans Affairs Blind Rehabilitation Center at Palo Alto, California, estimated that there were 93,000 blinded veterans in 1990. Estimates were based on data from the National Center for Health Statistics. Dr. Goodrich recently revised the figure to 100,800 based on additional data from the 1990 census. The blinded veteran population is predicted to grow to over 130,000 in the next ten years. The number of blinded veterans approaching BVA for help will certainly increase in years to come.

Chapter III: Signs Along the Way

In fact, most of our work today—the work we do at National Headquarters and in the field—is with older blinded veterans, men and women who returned home from military service, resumed their civilian lives, and are now losing their sight, or are blind because of age related eye diseases.

BVA has a toll-free telephone number that all blinded veterans, or anyone, including family members, can use to call us for help, night or day. Each morning when we open the office in Washington, D.C. we write down the recorded messages that have come in overnight. It's a time of some anxiety for those of us who take action on the calls. There are so many blinded veterans that call us for help. Often it's the spouses that call in asking if BVA can possibly be of assistance. Sometimes we ask ourselves how will we keep up with the calls for help. It's a very clear sign of things to come.

There are more signs that tell of obstacles and challenges ahead. Public perceptions of the capabilities of blind persons have not improved. In fact, we fear sometimes that we are sliding backward and that our efforts to tell Americans about blindness and what blind people can do may have failed. We find it more and more difficult, in spite of new laws such as the Americans with Disabilities Act, and others, to get employers to hire blinded veterans. The attitude seems to be that blind people can't compete with sighted workers, or don't need to work because the government takes care of them. Neither statement is true. Perhaps it's just what people want to believe in spite of being told and shown how it really is. Blinded veterans, blind people in general, can work and do good work, and blind people do need to work for the same reasons as sighted people. They need to work so they can earn money and support their families, and feel like they are a part of life in America. We've got to do more to get this message across. It is so important for the public to understand that most blinded veterans receive little or nothing from the government; perhaps only minimal assistance from Social Security. Most blinded veterans receive no financial help from the Veterans Administration. The status of the blind in America has not changed much at all. This is not a good sign.

Even as an increasing number of blinded veterans approach BVA for help, and even as BVA tries to do more with its limited resources, we see what we feel is an appalling lack of concern on the part of many Americans for veterans' problems, particularly health care.

One of the major activities of BVA is to represent blinded veterans before the U.S. Congress and the Department of Veterans Affairs as well as other government agencies. Our goal, as is the goal of other veterans service organizations, is to maintain support for veterans programs and express the continuing concerns of veterans. In our case, it's support for programs for blinded veterans—programs such as blind rehabilitation, visual impairment services, prosthetics, sensory aids, and financial assistance for poor veterans are key concerns. It is a never ending struggle just to hold on to the little we've been able to achieve.

Old friends and supporters leave Congress and the federal agencies, too, and new faces come on the scene with new agendas. The education process must continually begin anew. It seems that as the memory and

Chapter III: Signs Along the Way

pain of war recedes, so does our nation's support for veterans. At BVA we live with the pain and the memories each and every day, and we cannot forget our nation's debt to veterans. So we keep on fighting. It's sad that many people won't remember or take the time to learn what America's veterans did for all of us. It's sad, but it's a sign.

Raising funds to support our programs is an increasingly difficult job. The Blinded Veterans Association receives no funding from the federal or state governments. What we are able to do to help blinded veterans depends entirely on the contributions of individual donors.

Our programs cost money, and increasingly so, as prices go up. Our major expense is operating our BVA Field Service Program. It's a good program. In an average year we will work one-on-one with over two thousand new blinded veterans and their families and provide continuing services to over twelve thousand blinded veterans. Our Field Service Program is not keeping up with the need, indeed the demands for help. We need to do more on all fronts: outreach, counseling, job development, referral to services, arranging health care and keeping the public better informed and educated on issues affecting the blind.

Preparing and sending out the *BVA BULLETIN* is an expensive proposition too, but it must be done. Blinded veterans rely on it for information on programs and services, and information on technology and adaptive equipment. They need to know what other blinded veterans are doing to cope with blindness and keep their families together. We send the *BVA BULLETIN* out six times each year in large print and tape cassette to nearly twenty thousand blinded veterans. If a blinded veteran doesn't receive his or her latest issue, we certainly hear about it. It's important, but it costs money and prices go up. It's not a good sign.

We need to fund more scholarships too. BVA currently offers twelve scholarships, each for two thousand dollars to the spouses and children of needy blinded veterans. The requests for the scholarships are numerous and we can only accommodate a few. It's difficult to turn deserving people down.

Research is another area that is vitally important but incredibly expensive. BVA is currently helping fund research on the optic nerve at Yale University. We know that what is learned through these research efforts will never help us individually, but it may help others in the future. A lot has been learned already like what happens when the optic nerve—the nerve bundle that transmits messages from the eye to the brain—is damaged, and the very brief period of time that exists before damage is permanent and irreversible. But each year, our BVA Board of Directors and our membership courageously and faithfully vote to keep alive the limited research effort we can afford. Research is expensive and results are slow in coming. It's not a good sign.

All the signs that involve money are not good. The challenge will be to find new ways to make sure the funds are there to keep our programs and services there for our blinded veterans. The challenge will be to plan carefully, to be innovative in the design and extension of our programs for blinded veterans to make every dollar count, and to take time to read all the signs.

The Blinded Veterans Association is fortunate in

having the skilled and dedicated leaders that are quite capable of reading the signs that tell of the road ahead. They are our "Team for the Times," the blinded veterans who are our National Officers and District Directors. You'll meet them in the next chapter.

Chapter IV: A Team for the Times

In the preceding chapter, we talked about the challenges ahead for the Blinded Veterans Association. In this chapter, we want to introduce you to the men and women who guide the Association and must meet the challenges of the coming years.

For nearly fifty years, BVA had been led and guided by blinded veterans serving as National Officers and District Directors, volunteering their time and often serving at their own expense. We have been fortunate. Blinded veterans dedicated to the mission and continuance of BVA have always stepped forward and volunteered to serve. We have been fortunate to have always had elected leaders with the vision, talents and skills to guide the Association through difficult times.

Our leaders are elected. Every year, at our BVA National Convention, BVA members elect a National President, a National Vice President, a National Secretary and a National Treasurer. BVA by-laws allow our National officers to serve two consecutive one-year terms. This system works well for BVA. A blinded veteran will often begin by standing for election for Treasurer and then, over time, stand for election to higher positions. This offers an excellent opportunity for the individual to gain experience and learn the traditions of the Association. This system is not mandated by BVA by-laws, but has served to produce experienced, knowledgeable leaders.

The National Officers, along with the District Directors and the immediate Past National President, make up the Board of Directors. The National President serves as Chairman of the Board of Directors. The National President appoints members of the Board to function as an Executive Committee, and appoints board members to serve on other committees of the Board. The BVA District Directors are elected at varying intervals by blinded veterans in the respective Districts. District Directors serve three-year terms before stepping down or standing for reelection. The Board of Directors holds two full meetings each year, and the Executive Committee of the Board will ordinarily meet twice a year. All National Officers and District Directors work without compensation. They are volunteers. They are all blinded veterans.

At BVA's 48th National Convention held in Tucson, Arizona in August 1993, the members elected a new slate of National Officers. We would like to have you meet them, and learn what each brings to the Blinded Veterans Association at this critical time in our history. We would also like to have you meet the Past National President and the District Directors who along with our National Officers comprise our Board of Directors.

Carl E. Foley is BVA's National President. Carl resides in Kettering, Ohio. He has held all BVA National Officer positions, has served as a BVA District Director, and has been active in BVA Regional Group activities, particularly in Ohio, Indiana and Michigan.

Carl served in the U.S. Air Force during the Korean War and was discharged due to service connected vision loss. After leaving the Air Force, he earned a bachelor's degree in mathematics from Anderson University, Anderson, Indiana and a Masters degree from the University of Oregon. Carl worked as a high school mathematics teacher in Indiana and Ohio until more vision loss forced him to end his teaching career.

After blind rehabilitation, Carl then began a twenty year career as a businessman, a distributor of adaptive equipment for the blind and visually impaired. He has acquired expert knowledge and professional capabilities in working with adaptive equipment for the blind and visually impaired that is truly remarkable. Carl has special knowledge, too, of computers and computer adaptations that accommodate blindness and low vision.

Helping the blind and visually impaired was more than just a business to Carl. He has been active in local, state, and national organizations for the blind and persons with low vision, and has held offices in many of these organizations.

As National President, Carl has set definite goals that

Chapter IV: A Team for the Times

he believes BVA can achieve during his tenure. His goals center on blinded veterans and the role BVA can play in helping them help themselves. He believes strongly that blind and visually impaired people can lead full and successful lives with a little help, and that BVA's role is to help them help themselves.

Carl is quick to express concern about the increased workload facing BVA because of more veterans becoming blind or visually impaired through eye diseases as the veteran population ages. He sees this as one of BVA's most critical challenges. "Planning is going to be critically important, so BVA can help the thousands of veterans who will need us. We need more Field Service Representatives to find and help blinded veterans. It's a real problem. Blinded veterans look to us for help. There is no one else for them to turn to. This is what I see as the major challenge and the goal I want to achieve—finding the resources that will let us do the job we must do."

Gerard M. McDonnell is BVA's immediate Past National President and a member of the BVA Board of Directors. "Jerry" was BVA National President from 1990 to 1993, and previously served as National Vice President, National Secretary, and National Treasurer. He has been active with the BVA New York State Regional Group, and served as Regional Group President.

Jerry served in Europe with the U.S. Air Force, and was there during the Berlin Wall crisis, working as a medical technician in a military hospital. He lost his sight while in the Air Force due to a neurological disorder. He is totally blind.

Jerry earned a BA degree in history from Iona College in New Rochelle, New York, and an MS in guidance and counseling from Long Island University. He has worked many years for the Department of Veterans Affairs, first as a veterans benefits counselor and, for the past fourteen years, as a counseling psychologist in vocational rehabilitation at the VA Regional Office in New York City.

Bobby Ridener is BVA's National Vice President. Bobby served in Korea with the U.S. Marine Corps from 1950 to 1952. He is a blinded veteran who lost his sight to diabetic retinopathy.

Bobby served as BVA National Secretary, National Treasurer, and as BVA's National Sergeant-at-Arms. He has been active in the Tennessee BVA Regional Group, and has served as the Group's President.

Bobby worked for many years for a clothing manufacturer in Knoxville, Tennessee as a shipping supervisor, overseeing the work of a staff of thirty employees. He retired in 1978 after losing his sight totally, and attended the VA Blind Rehabilitation Program at Hines, Illinois.

Bobby has served as a member of the board of a land development company, and has been appointed Colonel Aide-de-Camp by two Tennessee Governors.

Bobby is an accredited Volunteer National Service Officer and works as a volunteer, helping blinded veterans obtain health care and blind rehabilitation services.

[Bobby Ridener passed away while this book was being prepared. He cared for blinded veterans and we will miss him very much.]

Elizabeth R. Carr is BVA's National Secretary. Elizabeth Carr is the first woman to hold a BVA National Office, and previously served as National Treasurer. Elizabeth was in the U.S. Air Force from 1968 to 1970. She became legally blind while serving in the Air Force.

Elizabeth holds a BA, cum laude, from C.W. Post Center, Long Island University, in sociology and social work and an MA, cum laude, in public administration, from New York University.

Elizabeth has been active in veterans affairs since leaving the military service, and has worked hard to advance public awareness of the problems and needs of women veterans. She has been particularly active in the Blinded Veterans Association. She is the current President of the New York State BVA Regional Group. She has served on committees of the BVA

Board of Directors, most notably as Chairperson of the Long Range Planning Committee. In her home state of New York, Elizabeth serves as a member of the New York State Senate Advisory Committee on Veterans Affairs. Since 1984, Elizabeth has worked as an investigator for the New York State Education Office.

Robert L. Smith III is BVA's National Treasurer. "Bob" is legally blind, having lost his vision to an eye condition incurred while in military service. He served two years in the U.S. Army and three years in the U.S. Air Force. He left military service in 1956.

Bob holds a BA and an MBA from Mankato State University, Mankato, Minnesota. He has a Ph.D. in organization development from the Union Institute, Cincinnati, Ohio. He has worked as an arbitrator for labor management disputes, in personnel and labor relations, in family investment securities, and has been a college professor.

Bob is President of the Minnesota BVA Regional Group and served an appointed term as Director of BVA District II. He is an accredited Volunteer National Service Officer and also manages the Minneapolis BVA volunteer office.

Chapter IV: A Team for the Times

Jack Shapiro is BVA District I Director. Jack was recently appointed by the Board of Directors to serve the remainder of the term of David Schnair who passed away in July 1993.

Jack is a blinded veteran who served in the U.S. Army from 1941 to 1946. His blindness resulted from wounds received while fighting in Europe during World War II.

He holds a BS degree in social service, and has a thirty year work record at the Social Security Administration in New York City. Jack was a claims interviewer; he retired in 1981.

He has been a BVA member since the very beginning of the Association, and has served as Treasurer of the BVA New York State Regional Group for many years. Since his retirement, Jack has also worked regularly as a volunteer in the Regional Group's office in Manhattan.

Harold Keith Marshall is BVA District II Director. He previously served on the BVA Board of Directors as Associate Member Director. Keith served in the Army Air Force from 1943 to 1946. Keith is totally blind; he lost his sight to glaucoma.

He attended the American

Institute for Business in Des Moines, and then worked for the Bankers Trust Co. Keith was owner and operator of his own trucking company from 1946 to 1974, and then, for the next four years, worked for an oil and gas distributor.

Keith has been active in the BVA Iowa Regional Group, and in local, state and national civic and service organizations. He has been especially involved in developing talking book and reading machine programs.

Ellsworth L. Sharpe is BVA District III Director. "Skip," as he is called by his fellow blinded veterans, was an Air Force pilot who flew military jet fighters. He left the military service in 1960 with onset of blindness.

Skip attended the University of Massachusetts and earned a BS in mechanical engineering. He also earned a Masters degree in education, and completed course work on a Masters in mechanical engineering.

Skip has been continuously active in BVA. He has served as BVA National President and in other National positions. He remains particularly active in the BVA Maryland-District of Columbia-Virginia Regional Group.

Skip worked for many years as an engineer with the National Aeronautics and Space Administration assigned to the lunar landing program. He is currently employed as a research engineer with the U.S. Food and Drug Administration. He is the guiding spirit and driving force behind BVA's support of research on the optic nerve now underway at Yale University.

David M. Szumowski is BVA's District IV Director. David was blinded totally in 1969 while serving with the U.S. Army in Vietnam. David has been continuously active in BVA affairs, and has served as BVA's National President. He also served as Executive Director of the Vietnam Veterans Leadership Program in San Diego County.

He attended the University of Richmond, where he was a distinguished ROTC graduate in 1967. He served in Vietnam as a 1st lieutenant with the 11th Armored Cavalry Regiment.

David received a J.D. degree from the University of Denver Law School, and worked four years as a veterans benefits counselor at the Veterans Administration. He then began practicing law. He began his current work in 1986, and is now the Deputy District Attorney for San Diego County in California.

George Stocking is BVA's Director of District V. George entered the U.S. Air Force after graduating from college. He trained as a jet pilot and then served as a flying instructor. He was injured and blinded in a mid-air collision. He underwent ten years of plastic surgery, with 111 operations.

George earned an MS in 1968 from the University of Miami and was employed at the Veterans Administration as a vocational rehabilitation counselor. He earned an Ed.D. in 1970 from the University of Miami and is now a rehabilitation psychologist at the Miami VA Medical Center.

Dr. George Stocking has been extremely active in BVA. He served as District Director for many years. He has been the inspiration and driving force behind the Florida BVA Regional Group and has held all offices in the Regional Group. George has been the editor of the Florida Regional Group newsletter for over 16 years.

John McDowell is BVA's Director of District VI. John is a veteran of World War II, and served with the U.S. Marine Corps from 1942 to 1944. He was totally blinded in the fighting in New Britain in the Pacific.

John attended college in Tennessee, and also attended Arkansas State Teachers College, receiving a BS in 1954.

For several years, John was self-employed as a rancher and restaurant owner and then attended Baylor University where he earned an MS in education in 1973.

John has served as District Director and member of the Board for over 17 years. He has worked very hard to organize BVA Regional Groups in the District he oversees and, as an accredited Volunteer National Service Officer, he is always on the job, helping other blinded veterans.

We have been able to tell you only part of the backgrounds and only some of the accomplishments of the blinded veterans who serve as our National Officers and District Directors. All have accomplished much and experienced much. Each has served our nation bravely and loyally, in military uniform, several in combat or in extremely dangerous assignments. Each has experienced the anguish of blindness or severe vision loss. Each has risen above adversity and struggled to be independent. Each has benefitted from the work and accomplishments of blinded veterans who went before. Each is an individual with individual skills and talents.

All are blinded veterans, and the very best role models for veterans who may one day be blind.

Yet, more importantly, they are a team. They work as a team, going about their work of directing and guiding the Blinded Veterans Association without reference to their own blindness or their continuing personal struggles. They are friends, and friends of blinded veterans, and their strength is in their common commitment to blinded veterans. And they can read the signs; they are a Team for the Times.

Chapter V: Families and Children

"When my husband lost his sight, I tried my best to understand how he felt and what he was going through. I know he felt alone and insecure. So did I. But there was so much that I didn't know or understand. It would have saved us both a lot of heartache and grief if someone could have told me what was going on inside of him, and me, too. We really should have seen a family counselor or found a family support group. I had the terrible feeling inside that now I'm trapped, this is going to change everything. I didn't know how to handle that.

"I remember that our families tried to help, but they didn't or couldn't realize what we were going through, and I couldn't tell them what I really needed. I didn't know myself. They did help us out with money and I appreciate that, but at the time it seemed as if they were rewarding me or paying me for staying with him, for staying on the job. It made me feel even more trapped and isolated.

"My husband became terribly depressed and withdrawn. It got so bad that he wouldn't talk to me. It was as if I was the one to blame for all his troubles, as if I had caused his troubles. There were many, many times back then that I felt like walking out.

"We finally contacted BVA, and he got the chance to go to the Blind Rehabilitation Program at the VA Hospital in Hines, Illinois. That gave all of us a chance *to catch our breath. When he came home he was in better shape, but I am still in it alone. Blind rehabilitation is a good thing, but I wish the wives could go through blind rehabilitation too."*

Blindness can exact a terrible toll on the family. In this chapter, we want to share some of our experiences in working with blinded veterans and their families, and discuss some of the issues facing families, and children too, when the father, or mother, becomes blind.

The issues and concerns facing the family, as well as solutions to the issues, are as complex as blindness itself. And there are real questions, too. Why do some families, when the spouse becomes blind, continue on and grow stronger, grow more compassionate and tolerant of each others' emotions and capacities, and learn how the family unit must interact in the new situation. And why do some families struggle unsuccessfully with the new stresses and pressures, stop communicating, begin to back away from one another, begin to compound each others' misery with bitterness, self-pity and self-justification and, finally, when the damage is irreparable, go their own ways. The answers are certainly in the questions.

The Blinded Veterans Association, as do other organizations, tries to deal directly with the problem of family instability through its outreach and counseling efforts. BVA has tried to examine the problem and gain a fuller understanding of what happens to other members of the family, when a spouse—in our experience, it's usually the husband, the father—becomes blind.

We have learned that a range of complex personal

Chapter V: Families and Children

and interpersonal issues are involved and must be addressed directly and indirectly when we work with the family of a blinded veteran. We have learned, too, that the process of recognizing and resolving issues endangering family stability is often lengthy and difficult.

BVA Field Service Representatives work one-on-one with blinded veterans and members of their families, as well as in support group meetings. The group meetings have proven an especially effective means for the spouses, generally speaking the wives of blinded veterans, to talk about the problems they are encountering and learn how other spouses are handling these difficult issues.

During support group meetings, the spouses are often quick in expressing the shock and dismay they felt and still feel about suddenly finding themselves with a blind husband who is deeply depressed, resists efforts to help him, refuses to help himself, and who appears to be intentionally isolating himself from his family and friends. This is what the onset of blindness can do.

Wives talk of the anger blinded husbands express toward them and the children, and the resentment they voice over the changed roles in the family and the diminished, dependent status the blind husband now believes is his. No longer being able to work, to drive the car, to see the children, to handle finances, to do home repairs, are some of the elements in the presumed diminished status. Matters of pride—male ego and self-identity, the male tradition of seeing oneself as being the head of the family—these too are often behind the anger and depression of the husband, and are often expressed in self-pity, bitterness and blaming.

Often the first reaction by family members to the husband's or father's blindness is to be brave, keep a stiff upper lip, be there for him at all times and to change their own lives to meet his new needs. It's a recipe for failure. Beneath the brave, assured, confident commitments lurks ignorance and fear, ignorance of the dangers of not doing things right, and the usually unspoken fear of what this situation will really do to the family.

The stories and the comments that family members relate to us are important in understanding the pressures that can break apart a marriage and destroy a family.

"We had been married for only a short time, only a little over a year when my husband was blinded. He was a Marine, and we were married when he first went in. Then he was sent to Vietnam. In 1967 he was wounded, just four months after he got there. He was back home blind in early 1968. We tried to go on with life as before. A year later, our first daughter was born.

"My husband went through the VA Blind Rehabilitation Program shortly after he returned home. I drove him up to the VA hospital near Chicago. I remember a staff member at the Blind Rehabilitation Center telling me that when my husband finished the training, he could return home and resume a normal life.

"A normal life for him perhaps, but what about a normal life for me? The question was never raised. I realize now how important a question it was at that particular time. I did my best, and kept it going for seventeen years.

"For a long time my husband was still recovering from his terrible wounds, and I tried to support him as much as I could or knew how, and I tried to

encourage him to be independent—to learn to do things for himself and to help with the children.

"I felt under a lot of pressure to be perfect, to always be there for him. I was never able to explain or to get him to understand the stress I was feeling. He would not acknowledge the pressure I was under. It's hard for anyone who hasn't been there to understand what I mean.

"I guess the pressures came from trying to do everything I could so he wouldn't get frustrated or depressed at being blind. I think I paid a heavy emotional price for this.

"I had been working, but my husband finally found work and I took care of the home and the children. Much of my time was spent in getting him ready for work and getting him there and home again after work. I felt isolated and frustrated. I felt I had been forced to put my own life on hold for a new reality, one I hadn't planned and did not know how to cope with.

"I remember that in the late 1970s I joined a support group formed by BVA. It had been set up so the wives of blinded veterans could meet and talk and help support each other. I enjoyed it and was disappointed when the support group no longer met. We would share our problems and feelings and it helped a lot.

"I recall how surprised I was at how much frustration and resentment was expressed by some of the wives. Some of them had lived with blinded husbands for years. Their husbands were veterans of World War II and Korea. The wives felt that the war was never going to be over for them. They felt that the pressures and expectations of society and their families, to be all, forever, for their blind husbands, had resulted in their

having to put their own lives aside, and to be their husband's eyes through the rest of his and their lives. They felt they had been forced by everyone to bury their own dreams and hopes and their own identities, too. It was so sad that they felt that way. They seemed to feel guilty about expressing these feelings too. I felt like that. I felt like I had been injured and had never had the chance to cry about myself, or get someone to look at me and understand that I was still me.

"But I was supposed to be strong and not look at my own needs, whatever I felt them to be. It seemed wrong, at least I felt it was wrong to think of myself. We had never set limits or rules about how we would manage our daily lives so each of us could be a person. We had never set rules that let us talk about what we were feeling. We finally broke up. This is only part of what happened, but I think it was a major part of it. It might have been different if we had both realized early on that there are two individuals, two lives, two persons in a marriage and both need at least some independence and identity.

"What advice would I give to another person in such a situation? Just one thought. What others say you should do isn't necessarily right, and you must confront family pressures to give your life totally to someone else just because he is disabled. It's okay if it's your choice, but it should be your choice. Remember you are important too, and that you have a right to feel bad about things, and a right to grieve over what has happened to you. And if you are having a rough time, you too, deserve support."

BVA hopes that, in time, a network of family support groups may be established where spouses and other family members can communicate their problems and share their experiences. We hope that on some future day we can have such a network working for families, not just to deal with blindness issues, but for other issues as well—issues of concern to families such as health, education, social services and child guidance. We're working toward it.

The goal would be to set up a system that would support and strengthen the family in times of crisis. The fact is that many blinded veteran families break apart needlessly because the spouse, the wife, has no support system available.

We recognize that there are times when support group meetings cannot provide the special level of help that some blinded veteran families need in coping with particularly severe problems. Highly trained, highly skilled professionals, experienced in working with severe family dysfunction are required in situations where the blinded veteran's own emotional state is so precarious that, unless treated properly, there is little real hope for a stable family structure. At BVA, we see many such cases, often involving a blinded veteran suffering not only blindness, but also a set of symptoms, a syndrome called post-traumatic stress disorder, or PTSD.

One wife of a blinded Vietnam veteran remarked, *"My husband came back from Vietnam different. He came home blind, but that's not what I mean. He was given good care for his wounds and they sent him to a blind rehabilitation program, but until recently they just ignored his emotional problems. The doctors had him diagnosed as a neurotic. But now they say he has PTSD.*

"Even now, it's like he's living in his own dream world. It's a world where he doesn't have to think about his blindness or his other problems. It's a world I'm not part of, nor are the kids. It keeps us all at a distance from him. He's not even trying to cope with his blindness and won't admit to himself his life has changed. It's like he's stuck back there in Vietnam. We've done everything we can think of to help him, and he's been given a lot of help. He does know how to get around and do things for himself. Now I think the family should get some help, too. We certainly need it. If he can't change and is going to be that way forever, we need to learn how to live with it."

PTSD is often an unrecognized problem that affects the marriages and the families of blinded veterans. PTSD is not limited to veterans of the war in Vietnam, although much of the understanding of the problem has been gained since Vietnam. Indeed, many experts now agree that PTSD is a problem not limited to veterans of traumatic wartime or military experiences. It can occur whenever a person, a human being, is subjected to, or placed in, a traumatic situation. The traumatic situation can be physical or emotional, but it is a situation that a human being is not by nature equipped to experience or endure. Unrecognized and untreated, severe PTSD can essentially destroy the individual and have a devastating effect on the family structure.

In the past, the problem was often misdiagnosed or even dismissed as neurosis, or referred to as battle fatigue or shell shock. But the condition has now been very well observed, studied and documented, and it is now accepted that PTSD involves a specific set of symptoms, in whole or in part, a syndrome that can be described and identified.

Many of the family members who approach BVA for assistance, tell of a blinded veteran husband, father, or son who may be suffering PTSD. There are many symptoms, and it takes an expert professional to fully identify, diagnose and treat PTSD.

It is felt by experts in the field that untold thousands of people probably suffer from PTSD. The source of the disorder can be almost any severe traumatic experience or situation, such as a soldier's experiences in combat, a civilian being bombed during wartime, or being in a tornado or hurricane, or an earthquake. Emotional trauma can be the cause of PTSD, for example, child abuse and incest. It is now recognized that almost any life threatening situation that can cause severe, continuing anxiety, can and may result in the symptoms associated with the disorder called PTSD.

Many of the blinded Vietnam veterans we have worked with demonstrate the symptoms of PTSD—symptoms that pose a distinct threat to the stability of the family and sometime pose a potential physical threat to family members.

What are some of the symptoms we see among the blinded veterans we work with at BVA? We often recognize a reluctance on the part of the veteran to form and keep close relationships both within and outside of the family. The veteran often seems to be unable to concentrate. We note this by the veteran frequently dropping out of training programs, or not completing training, and being fired from jobs.

Other commonly cited symptoms of PTSD are episodes of extreme anxiety and panic attacks, sometimes accompanied by dizziness and muscle tension, particularly in the back muscles, and an increased heart rate. Very often we see evidence of drug or alcohol abuse, too. This problem often begins when the veteran tries to self-medicate to relieve the anxiety he feels. Many things seem to be able to trigger a panic attack, particularly events that can bring back the memory or mental picture of the traumatic event. The recollection can be conscious or unconscious.

Even dreams may trigger the panic attack and the veteran may wake up screaming or in a cold sweat. In such a panic attack, the veteran may become violent and pose a threat to family members. Veterans tell that a flashback—a sudden, visual recall of the traumatic event—can trigger a panic attack. Sounds, odors, even pictures can bring on extreme reactions. Veterans also tell of extreme nervousness and jumpiness, of being unable to relax and feeling they must always be on the alert. Another identifiable symptom of PTSD would be depression, or would be emotional numbing, paranoia, and the quite common feeling of guilt for having survived the traumatic situation while others did not.

There are more symptoms, too, such as intrusive and uncontrollable thoughts, and of course, the anger and resentment we discussed previously. Perhaps you can recognize some of these symptoms in the accounts of veterans' spouses. At BVA, we realize that the experience of being blinded, or going blind, is in itself traumatic. PTSD is an old and powerful enemy.

There is yet another aspect of PTSD that is usually unrecognized and rarely given appropriate treatment. It's what we often call "secondary PTSD." It happens when the veteran's symptoms leave their own traumatic imprint on members of the family. The symptoms can

Chapter V: Families and Children

be much the same as PTSD itself, differing only perhaps in severity. Drug and alcohol abuse, anger and resentment, depression, and verbal abuse by the spouse and children are often reported. All may be symptoms of secondary PTSD, and all have ruinous potential for the family.

We talked to one wife of a blinded Vietnam veteran who told us she had lived through it all. Her concerns were her three children.

"They needed help to be able to understand the stressful situation they were in. They needed to be shown how to develop respect for their father. They had been filled with anger over how he was reacting to them and had no respect for either of us. We were helped by the doctors at the VA hospital. They made us realize that we had to learn how to react effectively in our special situation and let him know we were supporting him and would be there for him. And we learned that it was alright to be members of the family of a blind person. I think the children needed to be let in on everything, which wasn't the case before. Kids need to know how to handle questions from other kids, and how to react to unkind comments. When they understood the total situation and how things were, they felt better. We learned what was causing the frustration and the stress and anxiety in our own lives, and he learned how he was affecting us too."

So, the fight goes on . . . to learn to understand and come to grips with the many issues of blindness affecting our families. We think the key for families is getting good advice and having the opportunity to meet and share experiences. As the wife of one blinded veteran remarked, "All I ever really needed from BVA was to be put in contact with another wife." Yet understanding blindness, what it does to the blind person and what it often does to the family, is certainly important too. The answer to problems in a family is always there, one merely needs to keep communicating.

Chapter VI: Filling the Ranks

"I joined BVA in 1986 just after I asked my doctor to help me so I could learn to live with my blindness and he said he had no idea how to help me. To me, BVA is the best thing that ever happened to blinded vets. From what I see, they go all out for blinded vets, and it's part of the effort. I've been a BVA volunteer since July 1988 and I want to give all the help I can to another blind person. I know what it's like to be blind and need help. I try to tell my fellow blinded vets, who are deeply depressed and have just given up, to try to keep on going, just keep at it and don't ever quit or give up.

"I try to serve as a role model for vets who have recently lost their sight. I am a World War II vet, and I'm totally blind, and it makes a difference when they see me up and around. I can share my experiences and what I've learned as a blind person and it really seems to help.

"I even walk them through the halls and up and down the stairs at the VA hospital where we have our BVA volunteer office. I show them what I can do and the things they will be able to do too. I show them how to use the elevators and find their way to the rest rooms and doctors offices, and generally how to get oriented when they're in the building.

"I am a BVA Volunteer National Service Officer. This

means the Department of Veterans Affairs has accredited me, given me the authority to help blinded veterans file claims for VA services and benefits. A lot of my work now involves helping blinded vets get their paperwork in. Sometimes I get frustrated at this part of my work because it takes so long to get claims processed through the system, but it's great when it finally gets finished and a blinded vet gets the help he needs.

"And even though I'm blind, I feel I've been blessed. I've been given a lot of help over the years. Now I have the chance to help someone else. Besides, it's fun and it gets me out of the house."

From Providence to Seattle, from San Diego to Tuskegee, all across the nation, blinded veterans are stepping forward and filling the ranks—volunteering—doing what they can to help their fellow blinded veterans.

Volunteering is in the very best tradition of the Blinded Veterans Association. BVA was organized and, in the beginning years, was operated by volunteers—blinded veterans determined to help other blinded veterans. Today, BVA's volunteers are critically important as we deploy our resources to meet the needs of the growing numbers of blinded veterans.

In earlier chapters, we talked of how the coming years will be a time of testing for BVA. Our veteran population is aging and thousands of veterans, men and women who served their country bravely and faithfully, will lose their sight through illness and eye diseases associated with aging.

Americans who served in World War II, Korea, as well as throughout the long years of the cold war will experience loss of sight and turn to the Blinded Veterans

Chapter VI: Filling the Ranks

Association for help. They will need help in coping with blindness caused by eye diseases with strange, unfamiliar names like macular degeneration, diabetic retinopathy, optic atrophy, glaucoma, and retinitis pigmentosa. The demands on BVA are great and will be greater still. We have found a way to help the many thousands of blinded veterans who now, and in future, will ask us for help. We will fill the ranks with volunteers.

Already we see a significant increase in the calls for help. We see it in the calls on BVA's toll-free number; in the growing numbers of calls to our Field Offices; and in the mounting numbers of referrals from VA Visual Impairment Services Team (VIST) Coordinators and community agencies. We must do more, and we think we have found the way through BVA's Volunteer Service Program. Volunteers are on the job, doing a good job in helping blinded veterans.

"I do it all. Whatever needs to be done. Most of all I like talking to a blinded vet who is having problems and needs someone to talk to. I do it mostly over the telephone. I know I'm helping," says Otho Cox, our BVA volunteer in Omaha, Nebraska. Otho is a retired Air Force veteran, and even though he's blind, he keeps the Omaha office going by himself, usually four days a week.

Like Otho Cox, blinded vets are doing their part and stepping forward to help—volunteering their time, sharing their knowledge and their own experiences, and reaching out to other vets struggling with the loneliness and despair of blindness.

Most of our volunteers are helping at BVA Regional Group Volunteer Offices in VA Medical Centers. They provide benefits information and counsel blinded veterans and members of their families too. An important task is to encourage new blinded veterans to enter a Blind Rehab Program and to take advantage of other services they may be able to get from the VA.

Some of our BVA volunteers live so far from VA hospitals, sometimes two hundred miles, that it would be impossible for them to travel to an office. These volunteers work from their homes. Dan Rozier is a good example. Dan is a BVA Volunteer National Service Officer and works from his home in Sioux Falls, South Dakota.

Dan spent twenty-one years in the Army; he's a retired first sergeant who had to leave the service because of vision loss due to retinitis pigmentosa. He has about two degrees of vision left in his visual field.

"I remember when I was at the Blind Rehabilitation Center. Most of the veterans were older vets who had really given up. I try to stay in touch with all the blinded veterans in the state after they get home from blind rehab and make sure they're practicing the things they learned. I try to find new blinded veterans too, and get them to sign up for blind rehabilitation. I know what I'm doing really helps."

Just talking and sharing with another veteran who has lost his or her sight is so important and means so much in getting through the crisis of blindness. It's something all blinded veterans can do, and do well. Many think that it's best for a blinded vet to talk to another blinded vet. They have all been through it, and sharing real experiences makes a real difference. Volunteers are also active in blinded vet support groups, leading meetings, and making sure that special issues and concerns on blindness are discussed and resolved.

BVA initiated a formal Volunteer Service Program in April 1992, as part of an overall effort to strengthen BVA Regional Groups and find a focus for Regional Group activities. For many years, volunteers had been an important part of the BVA service concept. In formalizing the Program, the BVA Board of Directors recognized the volunteers as a vital part of the mission to reach and help blinded veterans. Nowhere is this commitment to our mission more in evidence than in the work our volunteers are doing.

There are three categories of volunteers: the Volunteer National Service Officer, the Regional Group Volunteer and the BVA volunteers working through VA Voluntary Services, but no matter what the category and the duties are, it's all important work and there is an important volunteer job for everyone. Volunteers work varied hours. Most of the volunteers make it to the office one or two days a week, although some are there every day.

BVA now has twenty-five volunteer offices staffed by trained blinded veteran volunteers. Volunteers work in close association with BVA Field Service Representatives and their work is monitored by the Field Reps.

Some volunteers with special training and experience are "accredited" by the VA and are authorized to help blinded veterans file VA claims for services and benefits. They review claim files and analyze medical records, and even represent BVA and blinded veterans at VA hearings. These are BVA's Volunteer National Service Officers, or "VNSOs."

The Volunteer National Service Officers are BVA's most highly trained and experienced volunteers. They are all blinded veterans who have had, in some cases, decades of experience in helping other blinded veterans. In essence, they are qualified and capable of doing almost everything our Field Service Representatives do. They are BVA Service Officers.

A volunteer is accredited when we believe the individual has reached a high level of knowledge and expertise and is thoroughly familiar with VA and other programs and processes. At that point we will ask the VA to accredit the volunteer, that is, to recognize him as a Veterans Service Officer. VA will then authorize the volunteer to represent a blinded veteran through power of attorney, access official records, and perform all Service Officer functions related to prosecuting a veteran's claim.

Being a VNSO is a great responsibility. The VNSO, when possible, functions as the manager of the volunteer office and is required to work under the supervision of a BVA Field Service Representative and submit reports of his activities to BVA. We depend on the VNSO to exercise sound, independent judgement and provide professional assistance to his fellow blinded veterans. At the present time, we have thirty-five blinded veteran Volunteer National Service Officers on the job.

The Department of Veterans Affairs—we still refer to them as the VA—sets strict rules when it come to accrediting volunteers. Volunteers must be members of the veterans service organization they represent, must work a specific number of hours per year, and must have completed formal and on-the-job training. Accredited volunteers must also receive continuing training. We are proud that so many blinded veterans, many of them totally blind, are on the job as accredited volunteers.

Most of BVA's volunteers are not VNSOs, the majority are Regional Group volunteers and their work is equally important to blinded veterans and BVA. We now have over 100 blinded veteran Regional Group Volunteers on the job, either certified or in training. Regional Group Volunteers are members of their respective Regional Groups and recruited and nominated for their volunteer assignments, and the Regional Groups assist in providing needed financial and material support to the volunteer office. But, they are all BVA volunteers. They undergo the same training regimen as the VNSOs and receive BVA certification when they have completed formal and on-the-job training. They do not perform the "Service Officer" functions of the VNSO. However, many of the Regional Group Volunteers will eventually be accredited.

We put a great deal of effort into making sure volunteers are trained. Training starts with volunteers studying material on BVA and VA programs and services on tape cassettes sent out from BVA National Headquarters. Then the volunteers are given written tests to see what they've learned. At the same time we are receiving reports on the volunteers' progress at the volunteer office. If the volunteers pass the tests and on-the-job progress is satisfactory, then BVA awards certification, recognizing their achievement and ability to work with other blinded veterans.

There is one more category of BVA volunteer. In areas where BVA has been unable to open volunteer offices at a VA medical facility, blinded veterans come in to volunteer anyway. They work under the auspices of VA Voluntary Services and provide great assistance in helping patients around the hospitals, helping at mealtimes, delivering records, assisting in the various clinics, doing almost anything they can to help.

BVA volunteers enjoy their work. Helping someone else is always enjoyable. In a typical day, a volunteer may find himself at his desk working the telephones; talking with blinded veterans in his area; or talking with and counseling blinded veterans who come into the office. In many locations, blinded vets know where the volunteer office is located, and hospital personnel will also notify the volunteers when a blinded vet has come in for help or has been hospitalized.

It's especially rewarding to visit a sick veteran in his room and let him know there are people who know who he is and care how he's doing. Volunteers work closely with nursing staff to show them how to make sure blinded patients get help at mealtime and in taking their medications.

And, typically, a volunteer may spend the day trying to find help for a blinded veteran ineligible for help from the VA. We require our BVA volunteers to be experts on services and programs of other agencies in their communities, and to know how to get help from these agencies. It's one of the harder aspects of being a BVA volunteer.

A good day's work is convincing some frightened, hopeless blinded veteran to finally make the move to sign up for a Blind Rehabilitation Program. Many blinded veterans seem afraid to leave the known safety of their own homes and the support systems they know and face the personal challenge of going to a strange place by themselves. A volunteer who has been through this experience can often help the veteran get past the fear.

And, every day, a volunteer will have the opportunity to demonstrate the equipment and technology he uses to do his work. We have tried to equip our volunteer offices with up-to-date technology, adaptive devices and vision aids that the blind use in doing their work. This task remains to be fully accomplished. Equipment is expensive and much of what we use is donated or surplus. But the volunteers do a good job with what they have.

Most days will also find the volunteer helping the VA VIST Coordinators at the VA medical facility. In many locations, volunteers are proving to be of great help to the VIST Coordinators, helping blinded vets find the VIST office, answering telephones, calling veterans who didn't show up for appointments, and doing the "leg work" in escorting blinded veterans to the clinics. Volunteers also accompany the VIST Coordinator in making home visits to blinded veterans. By talking with another blinded veteran, the volunteer is often a major factor in getting a depressed, despairing blinded veteran to finally do something about the way his life is going. The BVA volunteers in Syracuse, New York, were recently able to get a blinded Vietnam veteran to leave his house and his self-imposed isolation and do something about his life after everyone else, the professionals that is, had tried for years and failed.

We ask our BVA volunteers to do more than just know what's going on in their communities, we ask them to be part of their communities. This means they have to get out of their offices to attend meetings, give talks, represent BVA at public hearings, write letters, go on radio and TV programs, and let the community know about the problems of the blind, what they are doing as volunteers. Our volunteers also enjoy this part of their work and do a fine job.

Providence, Rhode Island, is the site of our newest volunteer office. Larry Grant, BVA's Field Service Representative for the area, is trying to sign up the volunteers so we can maintain a five days per week operation. In addition to Providence, we are also opening volunteer offices in Buffalo and Syracuse, New York, and in Cincinnati, Ohio. And, in Omaha, Oakland, Seattle, Dallas, Albuquerque, Minneapolis, Manhattan, Tucson, Des Moines, in cities large and small, all across America blinded veteran volunteers are hard at work, helping their fellow blinded veterans. We are proud of them all.

Let us tell you our Philadelphia story. Sam Huhn, a blinded Marine; Chuck Groom, a blinded World War II Army veteran; Tom Brozena, a blinded Marine who served in Vietnam; and Al McFadden, a blinded Army veteran, operate the BVA Volunteer Office at the VA Regional Office.

Until a few years ago, BVA stationed a full-time Field Service Representative in Philadelphia. The Philadelphia area has an enormous population with many hundreds of blinded veterans. Unfortunately, funds to support the position were no longer available and we had to cut back. We could no longer afford to have paid staff assigned to the city and were preparing to close down the Philadelphia office entirely. One day shortly before we were scheduled to close the office, Sam Huhn came in and suggested he might be able to keep the office going with volunteers. Sam had been active with

Chapter VI: Filling the Ranks

the Pennsylvania Regional Group and had been a long time advocate for the blind in Philadelphia. He went ahead and recruited more blinded veterans to work as volunteers, and the Philadelphia office stayed open five days a week. Sam is now an accredited BVA Volunteer National Service Officer and, together with his fellow volunteers, provides a full range of services to blinded veterans in Philadelphia.

"The VA treats us really well," Sam told us. *"We are invited to meetings and training sessions, and given the same consideration and respect the other larger veterans service organization personnel are given. They know that even though we're blind, we can do the work we say we can do.*

"The Pennsylvania Regional Group has given us a lot of support too. They recently got us a good computer and a small printer and we're trying to get it to work with a voice synthesizer so the totally blind guys can use it. We also have a Closed Circuit TV system and tape recorders in the office. We are really getting set up to get a lot of work done."

The volunteers in Philadelphia have indeed filled the gap left when we had to withdraw the Field Rep. What better example can we give of blinded veteran volunteers filling the ranks?

In Tuskegee, Alabama, blinded veteran volunteers are carrying the load too. Andrew Dillard has been the driving spirit. He retired after thirty years in the U.S. Army. He's blind now, but that doesn't stop him. "Andy" is the manager of the BVA Volunteer Office at the VA Medical Center in Tuskegee, and along with Corwin Mathews, a blind veteran of the Army Reserve, and Hillard McAdoo, a blind retired Army veteran, runs a "shaped-up" office.

They have a tough job looking out for blinded veterans, many of whom are older veterans in long-term care at the hospital. The volunteers work the hospital rooms constantly, making sure that older blinded veterans, some of whom can't make their needs known, are getting the care they need. The volunteers at Tuskegee are known throughout the hospital. They work closely with the nursing staff and the physicians and the rehabilitation specialists to insure that they know what their blinded veteran patients need. The volunteers have made a difference; but they've had to be insistent on many occasions.

The volunteer office is open five days a week, and blinded veterans coming to the outpatient clinics routinely drop in at the office for a cup of coffee and to just hang out. That means they are going to get some on-the-spot counseling from the BVA "pros."

The Tuskegee volunteers are now pushing hard for an improved outpatient rehabilitation and training program for blinded vets who leave the hospital and return home. *"They need a place to come back to so we can make sure they are doing the things they have learned to do, and that they are not just sitting at home getting sick again,"* said one of the volunteers.

How can we put a price on the value of the work being done at Tuskegee by this small team of dedicated blinded veterans? And what would life be like for the blinded veteran patients at Tuskegee? We visited the hospital recently and watched as the BVA volunteers went about their work, walking the long halls with their white canes, chatting with the hospital staff, visiting blinded veterans lying in their beds — blinded veterans who rarely get other visitors—holding their hands, seeing what they needed, speaking words of fellowship and hope and of someday going home. Who can put a price on that?

San Diego, in so many ways, has been our model as we've worked to set up more volunteer offices. It's a model in the way it's organized and managed, and it's a model in the way the office has been given support and guidance by the San Diego BVA Regional Group.

Urban Miyares, a blinded Army veteran, is the Office Manager, and certainly an inspiration to the other volunteers that staff the office. Urban is an irrepressible optimist; his is a "can do' approach to any problem. Bill Montgomery, a blinded Navy veteran, serves as office supervisor and coordinates the work; and Frank Scarcella, a blinded Army veteran; Manuel Sorias, also a blinded Army veteran; Bill Hasse, a blinded World War II Army veteran; and Art Lucas, a blinded Air Force veteran, make up the rest of the team.

The San Diego volunteers specialize in reaching out to blinded veterans and getting them involved. They find ways to get them interested in being part of the effort to help other blinded veterans. San Diego is a city where the BVA volunteers capitalize on the California life-style, and have been particularly successful in getting blinded veterans out to picnics, social events, and recreational programs where they can meet other blinded veterans. It's San Diego's way of doing things and it works too. And if a blinded vet calls the office for help, the blinded vet gets help. The team goes to work on the problem.

All across America, blinded veterans, as a team or individually, are doing whatever they can to help a fellow blinded veteran. There is a way to meet the challenge of the years ahead, to continue our mission to help one another. Volunteers are filling the ranks.

Chapter VII: Getting to Know Blind People

George Brummell is BVA's Field Service Representative for the Mid-Atlantic States area. George is a Vietnam veteran and was blinded, totally, in the war. We were talking on the telephone one day: George was getting ready to go out of town on personal business. He lives alone, and was waiting for some sighted friends to come and pick him up.

Our conversation turned to our enjoyment of our sighted friends, and how much they mean to us. George had some interesting insights on the subject, and told me, *"I'm fortunate in having many sighted friends, nice friends, they're fun to be with and very helpful. I know they enjoy being with me, too. I wish more blind people could have this. It's sad, but many blind people are isolated and withdrawn, and the few contacts they have are with other blind people. Perhaps it's a result of everything that's happened to them. Most of the blind people I know are really interesting people and have a lot to give and share in a friendship. I wish sighted people, and blind people too, would make an effort to extend themselves to one another. Mostly, I wish more sighted people would take the time to get to know blind people. It would make everyone's life fuller and more enjoyable."*

Basic attitudes and perceptions, myths and misconceptions about blindness and blind people; fear of blindness and that uneasy feeling of not knowing what to do or say that some people have when they are around blind people, all of these factors serve to keep us apart.

We need to find ways to bridge the gap between sighted people and blind people. A way to begin is to remember that blind people are just people like anyone and everyone else. If we are different in any way, it's only that we've had to learn to get along without sight; and to adapt and cope with the situation. Blind people ask only to be accepted; and sighted people need only to acknowledge and understand blindness for what it is, a limitation. We need to remember too, that blindness is neither mysterious nor contagious.

In this chapter we want to look at some of the basic attitudes and misconceptions about blindness and blind people, and discuss some of the techniques we can keep in mind and use when working, meeting, just interacting with blind people. We will share some tips on blindness that have proven especially helpful, which will demonstrate how basically simple and easy it is to be helpful and at ease when one is with blind people.

First, let's look at a few assumptions and attitudes about blindness and blind people that many people have. For example, do you think it is possible for a sighted person to understand how it feels to be blind? If a person takes the time to learn about blindness and how a blind person copes, then it is possible to gain a good amount of understanding. Yet, in thinking about this question, we need to remember that blindness, to a blind person, is more than just not being able to see. There are many losses, personal losses, other than mere sight. Blindness is a personal, unending experience. One cannot understand blindness simply by closing one's eyes,

Chapter VII: Getting to Know Blind People

and imagining how it would be. Perhaps it's best not to worry too much about "understanding" how it feels to be blind, but to try to learn how to interact effectively with blind people. It's more important to just accept blind people as people. No one can really know or understand what it's like to be another person.

If a blind person could somehow get his sight back, would he then have a happy life? This is an easy one. Happiness rarely depends on how well our eyes, or other parts of our body work; happiness usually depends on our relationships with other people.

Do you think sighted people generally dislike being with blind people because they are blind? Not really, it's usually because they know so little about blindness that they don't know how or what to do when interacting with a blind person. An artificial barrier seems to exist which makes sighted people sometimes draw away. Somehow, if we can't make eye contact with another person, we feel strangely ill at ease. It's interesting why that happens. It's something we've been conditioned to do throughout our lives and when we can't relate to people through eye contact, we sense a barrier. The barrier is really our fears and false perceptions.

In view of all the wonderful new high tech adaptive equipment now available to the blind, do you think that blindness is no longer a handicap? Strangely enough, some blind people will insist this is the case, not only because of new adaptive equipment, but because of the coping skills they have acquired through training and rehabilitation. Much of the new equipment is oriented toward work and daily living activities, such as reading machines and other devices that can talk, and they are of immense help. Moreover, some blind people have developed truly amazing mobility skills. But the fact remains that the loss of any of our special senses creates a handicap, limiting us, often isolating us, requiring us to make changes in our lives, forcing us to find ways to cope, and setting us apart from the greater part of society. Blindness is a handicap, though the limitations need not be incapacitating. It depends on the person, and the reactions of other people.

If you lose your sight, should you just accept that your ambitions and dreams have to be abandoned, and not expect to have a happy life? That's how it often was in the past. Blind people were thought of as having no future, of being dependent and incapable, doomed to a life of tragedy and sorrow. This belief, by both the sighted and the blind, was often self-fulfilling, and when a person first becomes blind, it is natural to feel that way. But the statement is not true; most blind people can and do eventually lead happy lives and realize their ambitions and dreams after some adjustments are made. All it takes is some time and some help along the way.

Do you think blindness is a punishment for doing wrong, because the person has sinned? Again, it's incredible, but we still hear this being expressed. Moreover, when a person first loses his sight it is not unusual for him to wonder if God is punishing him. It's based on a fear of blindness, a fear so intense that one cannot look upon blindness as just another disability. Even today people still look upon blindness with such horror and see the situation as so horrible, so ghastly, that it must be a curse. Most blind people will tell you there are many things worse than being blind,

Chapter VII: Getting to Know Blind People

and the fear and mystery of blindness will fade as one learns more about it.

Is being blind better than having to see all the ugliness in the world? This is often asserted by sighted people to make blind people and themselves feel better about blindness. To blind people, such a statement is specious nonsense. One of the most acutely felt losses of blindness is no longer being able to see the beautiful, one's children or one's spouse, or look at pictures and see the wonders of nature. There are no benefits in losing one's sight. And, moreover, the ugliness in the world doesn't seem to bother too many people.

Do you think miraculous cures of blindness are possible? The quick answer is yes, and of course it's a matter of faith. We have all prayed for the miracle that would restore our sight to us, or that we may lose no more sight. Many of us have been admonished by family members, and complete strangers too, that if we prayed harder our sight would be restored to us. Yet, would one pray for a missing arm or missing leg to miraculously reappear, or tell an amputee to pray that his leg may be given back to him? People think this about blindness because it appears so mysterious and unbearably horrible that it must be due to some problem that needs Divine attention. It is the fear and ignorance of blindness that gives rise to the question.

A major part of the problem sighted people encounter when interacting with blind people seems to be centered on, "How do I do it? I feel ill at ease because I don't know the proper things to do. I'm afraid I won't communicate properly and will offend the blind person, so I just don't get into it." It's really not that difficult, one needs only to learn what's best to do. Almost everything you need to remember when interacting with blind people is based on common sense and common courtesy. These are some good techniques and approaches to keep in mind:

*Offer assistance to a blind person if you think he may need help. Just ask, "May I be of help?" and don't be hurt if you receive a "No." Remember, blind people try to be independent and use the skills they have learned. When you offer assistance to a blind person, speak directly to him so he will know you are talking to him and will be able to locate you. Speak in a normal tone of voice and don't shout. He's blind, not deaf.

*When meeting a blind person you may have met before, don't play, "Guess who?" Let him know who you are unless you are sure he knows your voice. Identify yourself with a casual greeting when entering a room occupied by a blind person. And please don't offend a blind person by addressing him through a third party. Incredibly, people still do this. And if a blind person extends his hand after being introduced, by all means shake hands. It feels terrible to have your hand out there, dangling in the air, because you can't see to take the other person's hand.

*It's okay to say, "How good to see you." and to use other phrases and words that imply sight. Blind people are not offended by such references, and would feel awkward if such normal words were avoided. So, it's okay to say, "I'll be seeing you" when you say goodbye. It's also okay to ask a blind person what he can see, that is, if you are trying to be helpful and not just curious. You can ask, "Can you read signs?" or "Can you read large print?" or "Would a magnifier help at all?" When properly asked, the questions show

Chapter VII: Getting to Know Blind People

proper concern.

*Don't be disrespectful or take advantage of a blind person by communicating around him through gestures and signs to a third person. Shaking and nodding your head "Yes" or "No" is also of little use in communicating with the blind person. Acknowledge a blind person's questions verbally since he cannot see a head shake or gesture.

*When you leave the room, or walk away from a blind person, tell him you are leaving. All too often a blind person is left talking into thin air, assuming a person is still near him or in the room. It's quite embarrassing and frustrating continuing to talk to someone who is no longer there.

*Interacting with blind people calls for some safety sense too. Blind people count on things being in their places, like chairs, footstools, and other items of furniture. If not left in their usual places, these items may be hazardous and cause nasty falls. And don't move a blind person's belongings from the place he normally keeps them. He'll have a hard time finding them again. Cabinet doors and doors in general are a hazard to blind people. Keep them closed so blind people won't bang into them. And if you see a blind person in a potentially dangerous situation, warn him and offer assistance.

*Guiding a blind person is easy, too. For example, when guiding a blind person across a busy street, permit him to take your arm. A nice way is to offer him your arm and say, "Here's my left arm," or, "Here's my right arm." The blind person will take your arm just above the elbow and will be able to follow your lead. Never grab a blind person's arm and try to push or pull him. Blind people find this particularly upsetting, not knowing what is in front of them. Imagine being pushed or dragged down a flight of stairs. It's an experience. Just let him take your arm and he will follow.

*When walking with a blind person, proceed at a normal pace; hesitate slightly before stepping up or down; and don't drag the blind person over curbs. Let the blind person know when you come to a curb, or are preparing to go up or down stairs.

*After crossing a street, make sure the blind person is started straight, in the right direction, and caution him about any unusual obstructions in his path. If you need to give directions, don't point; give explicit directions. For example, "Go three blocks straight ahead, cross the third intersection, then turn left two and a half blocks, and the building is on your right." Don't identify intersections by street names; blind people can't read signs. And don't use phrases such as "over there" in giving directions.

*In familiarizing a blind person with a room, you should tell him what kind of room it is: bedroom, kitchen, living room, etc., and what its general shape is: square, rectangular, etc. This helps to give him an idea of what to expect when traveling within the room. It is very important to let him know where the doors are: at the middle of the wall or at the end of the room. This establishes his relative position in the room. The door should always be used as a reference point, so the blind person can understand relative positions of objects within the room with respect to the location of the door.

*When showing a blind person to a chair, place his hand upon the back of the chair. Don't try to push him down into the chair. Another good way is to say, "Here's a chair," and place your hand on the back of the chair. He will slide his hand down your arm to the back of the chair.

*Dining with a blind person is an easy, enjoyable experience, too. It's fun to describe the restaurant decor and explain what's on the menu. Tell the blind person where things are on the table, and let him know when food is served. You can use the handy "o'clock" method to help him locate specific items. For example, you can say, "Your water is at 2:00 o'clock, or your bread is at 9:00 o'clock." You can offer to serve food from platters, and to cut his steak, too. With just a little assistance, dining out is fun for everyone.

*Don't assume that a blind person is unable to participate in any particular activity. Let the person make the decision, but extend the invitation. Most blind persons enjoy doing the things sighted people do, such as sightseeing, going to the movies, watching TV, and "seeing" friends.

*And please, don't ever express pity to a blind person. It's embarrassing and unwarranted and sets up a barrier to any real relationship between you and the blind person. And, don't exclaim "wonderful" or "marvelous" simply because a blind person can do an ordinary task such as telling time on his watch. Offer understanding, consideration, and friendship to a blind person; never pity or unwarranted praise.

*So, relax, and remember that interacting with blind people is rewarding, although it may be challenging at times. Do your best and don't be afraid of making mistakes. By all means, don't forget your sense of humor. Most blind people you meet will want to share your sense of humor with you.

Many of the blind people you will meet will use a white cane to aid in mobility. The white cane serves many purposes. Primarily, it serves as an extension of the person's arm. An incredible amount of information can be gained when the cane is used properly. In the hands of a skilled user, the cane can insure that the path ahead is clear and unimpeded; tell the type of surface the person is walking on; and detect and help identify doors, doorways, curbs, stairs, and furniture. It's also a warning sign, letting sighted people, particularly drivers, know that the person is blind.

Some of the blind people you will meet use dog guides to help them travel. Dog guide is the proper term, not for instance, "seeing eye dog" or "guide dog." These latter two terms are trademark names used by specific agencies that train and supply dog guides for the blind. Don't be afraid of dog guides. They are specially selected, and they are all quite friendly and like being around people. However, that's where friendship between you and the dog guide should end. There are some good rules to keep in mind when you are with a blind person who uses a dog guide:

– When the blind person is holding the dog's harness, it means the dog is working. It's best not to speak, pet or play with the dog at any time, but particularly when the dog is working and may be distracted.

– When assisting a blind person who is using a dog guide, let the blind person decide if he wants to use the dog and follow you, or relax the dog's harness and take your arm.

– Occasionally, sighted people will try to give commands to a dog guide, even when it's not working. It's

Chapter VII: Getting to Know Blind People

the blind person's responsibility to give commands. The dog may become confused if you interfere.

–If you see a dog guide do something inappropriate, such as taking the blind person too near a dangerous place, growling and baring his teeth, relieving himself indoors, or taking food from a table, quietly tell the blind person so the problem can be corrected. As you meet blind people, you will also meet dog guides at various levels of age and training, and such things may occasionally happen.

–Don't be shocked if you see a blind person rather harshly reprimanding or correcting his dog guide. Dog guide users entrust their safety—indeed their lives—to their dogs and must immediately and strongly correct them when they do something inappropriate.

Many of the blind people you will meet use braille when reading or taking notes. Have one of your new blind friends show you how the system works. It's really interesting and easily understood. Braille is a method of writing the alphabet, numbers, word contractions and punctuation marks using a system of raised dots. Everything is based on a "cell," a six dot matrix. However, when writing braille by hand, it has to be done backwards since the blind person has to punch in the dots and then turn the paper over to read the words. Some blind people use mechanical or electronic braille writers and note takers. They range from old mechanical "braillers" to new high tech devices that can be carried in one's pocket, and can even be linked to a computer or a printer. Your blind friends may also show you a variety of interesting support devices they use, such as talking watches, and talking calculators, white canes which emit laser signals and sound an alarm when there is an obstacle in the path, and many others.

Remember too that some of the blind people you will meet may not wear dark glasses, and may not use white canes, dog guides, or braille. These people may or may not, have some usable vision, but the same rules of courtesy and common sense apply as with any person who is blind. A different level of assistance may be needed, but it will still be appreciated.

And that brings us to another issue, how do we interact with people who are at the higher levels of "legal blindness" or have what we call "low vision" or are "partially sighted?" These people have some sight and it varies from person to person, and often from time to time.

Some individuals who are legally blind may have adequate vision for traveling, or recognizing people. They may, however, need your assistance in reading a sign, crossing a busy street or reading items in dim light. When writing something for a person with low vision, write in large print using a dark pen or marker, if possible, so the person can read it more easily. And, much like a totally blind person, a person with low vision will do better in familiar surroundings, where he knows where things are and can find what he needs.

Reading is always a problem for people with low vision. They often benefit by using closed circuit TV systems if they are able to afford them, or they will use strong magnifying lenses along with large print materials. But it's always a problem, and people with low vision appreciate help in reading. Lighting contrast is important too. There are so many variations of low vision effect that it is impossible to give any set rules on lighting contrast, but usually bright light is better. Ask a friend with low vision what is best for him.

Fatigue and stress are often serious problems for a person with low vision, one who is partially sighted. Seeing often requires great effort for such persons, and much energy is expended in the effort. Fatigue, physical stress, as well as illness may affect the person's vision level and his ability to use remaining vision. Be sensitive to the fatigue factor that may affect some of your friends with low vision. And, remember, by the time we reach age sixty-five, all of us will have lost at least some of our useful vision. Many of us will lose a great deal more.

Gaining new friends who are blind, and just interacting with blind people can be a rewarding and enjoyable experience. Blind people have much to share and value friendships; and, in a sense, overcome blindness when they are accepted and treated with warmth and dignity.

Chapter VIII: I'm Worried Doctor

"I'm worried Doctor, I'm not seeing well. I think something's wrong with my eyes."

Those are words we hope you will never have to say. Yet, thousands of Americans make similar statements to their doctors every year. Eye diseases are on the increase as America's population ages. At BVA, nearly seventy percent of the new blinded veterans we are now trying to help have lost their sight through eye diseases.

While blindness from combat wounds and injuries suffered during military service still account for the blinding of many veterans, and accidents and injuries in civilian life account for more, a majority of blinded veterans whose names are in our files, have lost their sight through diseases that affect the American population as a whole. We are all at risk.

In this chapter, we want to talk about some of the more common and prevalent eye diseases, conditions that cause blindness or severe vision loss, conditions which are sometimes preventable, but more often are not.

We want to explore some of the symptoms and the course of these eye diseases, and talk about the vision loss that may occur as well as what we may do to in terms of prevention. And we want to talk about adjusting to blindness or severe vision loss, and about some of the new technology and adaptive equipment that may help.

Chapter VIII: I'm Worried Doctor

We can only share what we have learned through our own experiences. We are not physicians nor are we ophthalmologists; we can talk only in layman's language, and share what we know, that you also may know the dangers and the warning signs of the major eye diseases.

Blindness has differing aspects, different levels and varying meanings. A person is considered blind if he is "legally blind." Legal blindness is just that, the point at which a person's vision in the best eye, with corrective lenses, falls to 20/200. Normal vision would be 20/20. A person is also legally blind if the visual field in his best eye becomes restricted to twenty degrees or less. The calculations must be made by a vision specialist. Most of us have had our vision tested and are familiar with the procedure.

Every veteran BVA tries to assist is at least legally blind, although most are either totally blind or severely visually impaired. In many cases, the term "legal blindness" means very little once the person gets over the shock of being diagnosed as legally blind. Often a great deal of usable sight remains at this point, and we work as hard as we can to get the veteran to learn to make the very best use of any remaining sight he or she may have. We try to get the veteran to accept the situation and get on with life.

The effects of vision loss, legal blindness and even what we call total blindness are many and varied. Total blindness is usually thought of as having no sight at all, and in many cases this is true. Total blindness is also used to describe a situation where the person has no usable vision, but may be able to detect light and perceive motion, although only at very close range.

However, even with many totally blind persons, enough sight may remain to aid in mobility and orientation to surroundings. Even the smallest amount of sight is something to cherish and build upon. That's how we look at it.

Vision loss through eye disease can begin at the center of the eye—the macula, where we have the sharpest vision—or it can begin at the outer edges of the visual field, the periphery. It can strike randomly, at various parts of the retina—the light sensitive membranes at the back of the eye—and disease can attack the optic nerve—the bundle of nerve fibers that carry messages from the retina to the brain. Disease may attack almost any part of the structure of the eye and cause blindness or severe vision loss.

In the case of severe vision loss, the job is to work closely with medical specialists to control the eye disease, and find ways to make the best use of what vision remains. We can't just sit there and wait for the world to end. We have to grieve our loss and acknowledge that our lives have changed somewhat. Then we must get on to rehabilitation and rebuilding.

Sadly, when a person is labeled legally blind, it seems to have a serious, negative impact on perceptions of self, self-worth, and often results in bitterness and depression, and this is a very human and natural reaction. Any vision loss, no matter how slight, is disturbing; severe vision loss is devastating.

It takes time to recover from severe vision loss, whether it's becoming legally blind or totally blind. But going on, going ahead with life, is certainly possible. At BVA we see this happening every day.

There are many fine agencies and associations that

periodically send out good information on blindness and vision loss, eye diseases and prevention of blindness. We would encourage all of our readers to become as familiar as possible with the subject, and take the time to read materials they may receive. Reading up on the subject can take away a lot of the fear. Some people fear blindness so much they don't care to read about it.

Blindness can often be prevented or slowed, and the effects can often be mitigated. It's important to remember that all of us are at risk, and we shouldn't turn our backs on the possibility and let it slowly come upon us, refusing to acknowledge blindness until it is too late.

Diseases that destroy vision often develop slowly, silently, over months and even years. Often there is no pain or other warning signs. Even as vision fades, people often remain unaware of the loss. The changes are so gradual and our ability to compensate is so great that the disease may destroy significant vision before it is detected. We again urge you, our readers, to learn as much as possible about eye diseases and, of course, get your vision checked regularly. That's what's really important.

The human eye is one of the most complex organs of the body. It is possible to see when all parts of the eye work together as a unit. If there is trouble in any part of the eye, vision may be disturbed or destroyed. On the last page of this chapter, we've printed a cross section of the eye. You may wish to refer to it as we point out the various parts of the eye, and describe some of the more common eye diseases and vision disorders.

The following are some of the major parts of the eye.

The sclera is the white part of the eye that protects the delicate interior of the eye. The transparent covering on the front of the eye is called the cornea. It protects the front of the eye and lets light pass into the eye without distortion. The pupil—the black center of the outer eye—controls the amount of light that is allowed to enter the eye. The lens focuses the light that passes through the eye. Light travels through the vitreous—a clear jell-like substance which fills the eye—and forms an image on the retina, the light sensitive layers of cells lining the back of the eye. The retina contains complex nerve cells which convert light to electrical impulses and transmit them to the brain via the optic nerve. The image is then interpreted by the brain.

The brain, too, is part of our vision system. In fact we actually see in our brain, not in our eyes. Injuries, such as stroke or blows to the head, at the part of the brain that interprets messages from the optic nerve—the visual cortex—can also cause vision disorders and blindness.

At BVA we have encountered hundreds of different eye diseases and disorders. Some are extremely rare, some remain undiagnosed, but most fall into a few common types or groupings. We want to talk about some of the more common problems, the leading causes of blindness.

Macular degeneration

A leading cause of blindness, perhaps one of the most prevalent vision disorders that we encounter at the Blinded Veterans Association is macular degeneration. Because it seems to strike in the later years of life, it is often referred to as age related macular degeneration.

Nationally, it is the leading cause of blindness among individuals over sixty-five.

As we can see in the cross section of the eye, the macula is the most sensitive part of the retina. It's the part of the eye we use to distinguish fine details; we use it when we read, drive a car, or try to find an object we've dropped or misplaced and distinguish it from other objects.

There are a host of different causes and specific diseases and disorders which may affect the macula and result in macular degeneration. However, in most cases the consequences are similar; the light-sensitive cells in the macula die, and the person is left without central vision. In age related macular degeneration, it is common for one eye to be affected first, then after a certain period, the other eye will be affected also.

Some of the first symptoms of macular degeneration are blurring of vision in the central visual field accompanied by headaches and muscle tension that go with straining to see what is now difficult to see. Lights appear as less bright, and fine details appear faded. This becomes noticeable when trying to read fine print. When both eyes become affected this is especially noticeable.

Although central vision is gradually lost to macular degeneration, side vision—or peripheral vision—usually remains, although in many cases we have seen, side vision may become somewhat distorted. But most people retain usable side vision. It's something to build on.

Most people with age related macular degeneration have the form of the disease which develops slowly. It is called the "dry" form. However, the dry form may develop into the "wet" or neovascular form of the disease. The wet form of the disease may progress rapidly, nerve tissue in the macula may be destroyed within a period of a few weeks or months. Fortunately, this condition affects only a small percentage of people with age related macular degeneration.

The damage to the eye, the macula, caused by macular degeneration is irreversible, and there is at present no effective treatment which can significantly delay or reverse the effects of the disease. However, the course of some types of the disease may be slowed by laser treatment, particularly for those who have the "wet" form of the disease.

The important thing to remember is that most people with macular degeneration will continue to have significant usable vision throughout their lives, and may well be able to continue leading useful, productive lives. Extreme magnification of objects and printing is often the answer to the vision limitation imposed by macular degeneration. New technology, such as closed circuit TV systems which provide extreme magnification, often allow a person to read, continue hobbies, and keep on working. Life does go on after macular degeneration, but it's a devastating form of vision loss. Some of the most depressed and withdrawn veterans we work with suffer from vision loss through this disease. It takes some time to adjust to it.

Diabetic retinopathy

Another disease we see too often at BVA is diabetic retinopathy. Many of our totally blind veterans have this disease, and it is one of the leading causes of all new cases of adult blindness.

Diabetic retinopathy is a complication of diabetes mellitus. It strikes the retina where the disease tends to cause blood vessels at the back of the eye to break and bleed into the normally clear fluid in the eyeball. Diabetic retinopathy may progress to the point where new, abnormal, and extremely fragile blood vessels begin to grow in the retina. The new blood vessels break easily and bleed into the eyeball. Vision is affected by the blood in the eyeball, and blindness occurs from hemorrhaging and the resultant scarring on the retina. Scar tissue may also detach the retina from the back of the eye causing permanent vision loss and blindness.

As you can see, it is extremely important for people with diabetes, or at risk for diabetes, to be especially vigilant and concerned about what may be going on in their eyes, and get frequent eye examinations. In many cases, diabetic retinopathy can be treated or slowed through laser treatment and medications, but only if it is treated at an early stage before the disease is significantly advanced and much vision is lost. The disease must be recognized early, before the damage is done.

Retinitis pigmentosa

Retinitis pigmentosa, or RP, is the name given to a group of diseases which affect the retina of the eye. In RP, the retina begins to degenerate, causing sight to gradually diminish. Unlike macular degeneration, where sight is lost at the center of the eye, RP causes sight to be lost on the periphery. Side vision is lost.

An early symptom of RP may be difficulty in seeing at night or in dimly lighted places. This is often followed by the loss of peripheral vision. The symptoms tend to increase over time, until only a small area of central vision remains. And eventually, even this small amount of remaining vision may be lost to RP.

We see many veterans with retinitis pigmentosa in our work at BVA. Until recently, the Department of Veterans Affairs was reluctant to assist RP veterans, insisting that the disease was an inherited disorder, and refusing to help veterans even if the disease developed while they were in the service. Fortunately, rules have changed and assistance is offered to veterans with service-connected RP. The disease is common among children and young adults, but as our experience shows, it can develop at any age.

RP is a particularly difficult form of blindness with which to cope. At the present time, there is no effective treatment for halting the course of the disease. Fortunately, vision aids have been developed, and the new adaptive equipment for the blind such as computers and reading machines with voice synthesizers offer considerable assistance in completing education, maintaining employment and coping with RP. Many blinded veterans with RP are still holding jobs and leading full lives thanks to the new technology.

Glaucoma

Glaucoma has been called the "sneak thief" of sight. The most common form, open angle glaucoma, remains undiscovered in nearly fifty percent of its victims until significant vision has been lost. The disease progresses silently presenting few symptoms. The loss of sight, usually side vision, is so gradual it often goes unnoticed.

Glaucoma is associated with a gradual elevation of fluid pressure within the eyeball which eventually destroys delicate fibers that lead to and make up the optic nerve.

Although this type of glaucoma can often be successfully controlled with medication and surgical procedures which may relieve fluid pressures, all too often the problem is discovered only after it has caused major, irreversible sight loss. Without treatment, the field of vision will gradually narrow, and vision may be permanently and totally lost.

People over the age of 40 are particularly susceptible to glaucoma, and we see many cases of blindness from glaucoma in the blinded veterans we help at BVA. And, too, there are other forms of glaucoma that may come on suddenly, at any age, and may be accompanied by pain, blurred vision and other symptoms. Blindness can come on quickly, too. It's most important to remember that the usual conditions leading to glaucoma—fluid pressure buildup in the eye—can be detected by a simple test given by your eye doctor. If there is a problem, treatment is available.

Cataract

Cataract occurs in the lens of the eye. The lens, which focuses the light, is usually clear to allow light to pass through without interference or obstruction. However, the lens may become clouded and opaque, and distort or block the passage of light into the eye, seriously affecting vision. The most common type of cataract seems to be, again, related to aging, although cataract can develop at any age.

Great strides have been made in treating many if not most cataract cases. Cataract usually develops slowly, and when a cataract progresses to the degree in which vision is seriously impaired, the lens of the eye is surgically removed and a lens implant is grafted in its place. In other cases a contact lens or special glasses may be prescribed. Cataract surgery is a common procedure and one of the most successful operations performed today. Some of us may remember that time when many of the "permanently" blind suffered from cataract.

Corneal diseases and disorders

Corneal diseases and disorders are another significant cause of blindness. As you can see in the picture of the eye, the cornea is a transparent coating which shields the front of the eye and allows light to pass through without distortion. Injuries or disease processes that result in clouding the cornea can result in partial or total sight loss. Wounds, blows to the eyes, chemical burns, and untreated eye infections can all cause severe damage to the cornea and impair vision.

If vision is severely impaired, a corneal transplant may be the only means by which sight may be restored. Corneal transplants involve surgical grafting of another human cornea, and are usually successful because the cornea has no blood supply and the transplanted cornea is not usually rejected by the body. However, healthy corneas from organ donors are often in short supply. It's something all of us can think about doing — being an organ donor — which is a wonderful thing to do. It may restore a fellow human's sight.

These are only a few of the diseases and disorders that can cause blindness. There are many, many more and, as you can see, there is often very little that can

Chapter VIII: I'm Worried Doctor

be done once vision is lost. Prevention of blindness is the only answer. Seeing an eye specialist regularly, protecting eyes from injuries, and being as knowledgeable as possible about eye diseases and their symptoms is part of the answer too.

There are many fine organizations you can contact for information and help: the American Foundation for the Blind, the American Council of the Blind, the Lions International, and the Society for the Prevention of Blindness, to name just a few. BVA can help too. We are always happy to share what we have learned to try to help.

It is our dream at BVA that one day no one will be blind and all eye diseases will be conquered. It is our dream, too, that some day a way may be found to help those who have lost their eyes completely.

We have tried to do more than just dream about it. We are trying to be part of the vitally important work that may someday allow us to replace or transplant major parts of the eye and restore sight to the blind. It's a dream, perhaps an impossible dream, but if you act, dreams can come true. As you can see by the cross section of the eye, the eye is somewhat like a camera, it picks up the visual image and transmits messages to the brain via the optic nerve.

For our part, we are doing our best to try to learn more about the optic nerve, not in the hope that some day eyes may be replaced, but that, in the short term, we may learn how to keep the optic nerve from being permanently damaged through injury or the disease processes we've talked about.

BVA has funded research on the optic nerve for six years. We give all we can. This year we managed to send $25,000 to Yale University to help fund the Research Fellow who is doing work on the optic nerve. It is difficult finding the funds to do this, and we know that the results of the research effort will not help any of us. Still, if we keep at it, we may learn important new information that will help future generations of Americans.

The research effort at Yale has focused on understanding the molecular changes that occur within retina nerve cells called ganglion cells and their nerve fibers called axons, which make up the optic nerve, as a result of various pathological injuries. The goal of the research program is two-fold. First, to develop therapies that will limit the amount of cell death in the visual system after trauma, and second, to develop treatment that will enhance recovery of function after injury to the visual system occurs. The researchers have already made important progress.

They continue to study mechanisms that lead, over an interval of hours, to the death, from trauma, of nerve fibers within the optic nerve. This process of secondary nerve cell death involves a "cascade of molecular mechanisms." Researchers have discovered that this molecular cascade can be interrupted at several points, suggesting that it may be possible to develop therapies which will limit nerve cell death, and thus promote recovery of function after trauma to the visual system. Several drugs, which block some of the chemical changes in nerves following trauma, have been studied. They are known to be relatively safe for use in humans.

The researchers have begun to study changes within retinal ganglion cells—the visual cells that give rise to nerve fibers within the optic nerve—and have detected the presence of specialized ion channels that admit calcium. Calcium is important in that following acute injury, the increased levels of calcium lead to nerve cell death. Yet, small increases in calcium may be involved in the regulation of nerve cell growth and regeneration. Researchers have found in fact that small increases in calcium within retinal ganglion cells can be amplified within the nucleus of the cell, and they believe that calcium within the nucleus may serve to turn on the process that initiates regeneration. Researchers feel this is an extremely exciting finding since it suggests that it may be possible to promote regrowth of axons within the optic nerve after injury by controlling the genetic chemical process.

Researchers have also begun to study the physiological effects of transplantation of special neural or glial cells into tracts of abnormal nerve fibers. The goal in these studies is to explore the feasibility of using neural transplantation as a mechanism for repairing injured nerve fibers in the optic nerve after trauma.

So . . . as you can see, research on the optic nerve is very complex, knowledge is gained slowly, and small gains build upon each other. But, we are encouraged and patient. The quest for new knowledge can be long, difficult and costly, yet it's so very important to press on.

It remains our dream, our hope, that one day there will be no more blindness. We are realists and know that the day, when it comes, must be in the distant future. In our time we will go on with our work, telling people about blindness and how it may be prevented and, if it comes, what blindness is and what it is not — that life can go on, full and independent.

Cross Section of the Eye

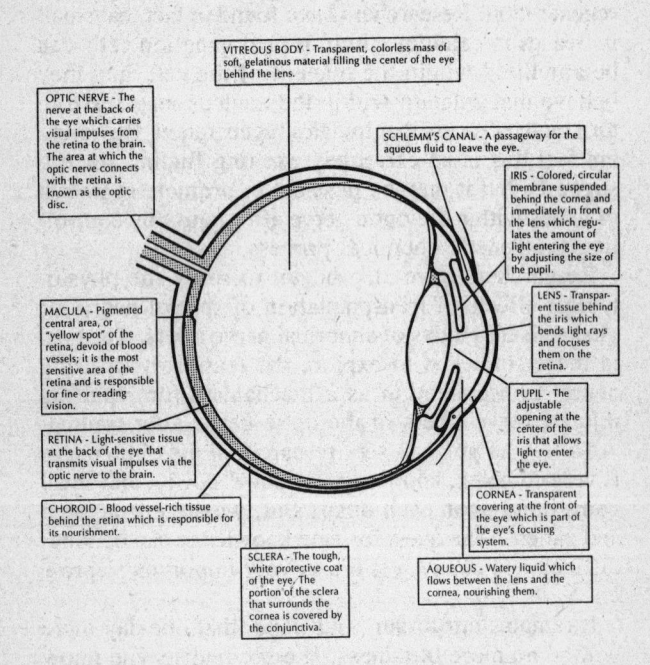

VITREOUS BODY - Transparent, colorless mass of soft, gelatinous material filling the center of the eye behind the lens.

OPTIC NERVE - The nerve at the back of the eye which carries visual impulses from the retina to the brain. The area at which the optic nerve connects with the retina is known as the optic disc.

SCHLEMM'S CANAL - A passageway for the aqueous fluid to leave the eye.

IRIS - Colored, circular membrane suspended behind the cornea and immediately in front of the lens which regulates the amount of light entering the eye by adjusting the size of the pupil.

MACULA - Pigmented central area, or "yellow spot" of the retina, devoid of blood vessels; it is the most sensitive area of the retina and is responsible for fine or reading vision.

LENS - Transparent tissue behind the iris which bends light rays and focuses them on the retina.

RETINA - Light-sensitive tissue at the back of the eye that transmits visual impulses via the optic nerve to the brain.

PUPIL - The adjustable opening at the center of the iris that allows light to enter the eye.

CHOROID - Blood vessel-rich tissue behind the retina which is responsible for its nourishment.

CORNEA - Transparent covering at the front of the eye which is part of the eye's focusing system.

SCLERA - The tough, white protective coat of the eye. The portion of the sclera that surrounds the cornea is covered by the conjunctiva.

AQUEOUS - Watery liquid which flows between the lens and the cornea, nourishing them.

Chapter IX: Standing with Us through the Years

Art Mathews is our BVA Field Rep in Chicago. Art was blinded in Vietnam and he has experienced all the heartaches and disappointments that a young blinded Marine can experience. He has also experienced the joy of being able to help another person, and is always on the phone with us, excitely telling, really celebrating, the good news that he has somehow managed to help another blinded veteran whom no one else would bother to try to help. Art is totally dedicated to his job, his personal mission of helping his fellow blinded veterans. It is not possible to hold him back. When he sees injustice and suffering, he goes right at the problem. Art wanted a chance to talk to the many friends of BVA who have kept him on the job, those whom Art sees as part of the BVA family.

"To me, a basic mission of BVA is to promote public understanding of who we are and what we can do as blind people; that we can make it in the sighted world with a little help and acceptance. We can be a part of our society and we don't have to be a burden. We just need a chance.

"I think we need to put more effort into getting this message out, but we need more resources. We need support from everyone who cares about what veterans have done for our country. Some of us lost more, some of us lost less, but we all did our best. People seem

to forget so easily and just turn their backs.

"If people would just back us up so we can get to those blinded vets who don't know about BVA and what we can do to help them. It's terrible when we find a blinded vet who has struggled on his own because we weren't able to reach him. It really frustrates me. It's more than just feeling frustrated, it really hurts when I know I haven't helped another blinded vet who really needed my help.

"I feel that to do the job that needs to be done, we need more Field Reps, and that takes greater public support and money. We've got to be stronger financially if we are going to be able to do more. I may be naive, but I think if the public just knew what we were trying to do, the support would be there.

"I wish people could have the chance to spend just a day with me and experience what I experience every day and see what I see every day. I wish they could listen to the scared voices, and hear men and women, blinded veterans, cry with relief when I'm able to help in even a little way.

"I wish that I had the time personally to do more of this—to tell the public about blindness and the job we do and what we haven't been able to do because we don't have the resources. I think if the public could just see me and hear me, they would understand what BVA has done for me and thousands of my fellow blinded vets. They've given me a future. I remember when I felt I had no future."

You, our special friends, have been at our side, standing with us through the years as we have struggled to keep our dream alive—the dream that we could somehow accomplish the immense task of finding and helping every suffering and struggling blinded veteran.

And even though our work is unfinished, even though the fight must go on, there is much we have accomplished together. Our gratitude cannot be adequately put into words. It's like trying to say thanks to your right hand, you are that close to us and that much a part of us. Yes, we are thankful and we do know the sacrifices you have made, often from your own limited resources, to show that you remember the service of all veterans and the terrible sacrifices, the terrible price paid by many. They thank you; we all thank you.

Now, I want to tell you of the things we have done together over the years and how BVA managed to stay in business because you cared and stood beside us through good times and bad.

When the Blinded Veterans Association was formed in 1945, it was truly only a dream—a dream formed in the minds of young blind soldiers and then written on paper by sighted friends. Sighted friends have played important roles in every aspect of BVA's development and continuance.

The young blinded soldiers dreamed that they could make the world a more bearable place for themselves and their blind comrades. They dreamed they could stay together, and work together and make the world a more bearable place for all blind people, and that someday blindness would no longer be an enduring tragedy.

And, in fact, most of those young men went on to lead the lives they had hoped for. Most went on to school, were married and raised families, and most found work and gave back to their communities. Many years have passed, and many of them are gone now, but the dream has endured and grown stronger now, thanks to you, our friends.

Looking back at those young men and their dreams and the formation of the BVA, one must wonder how they saw things, how they felt at the time, where they found the courage to form their own association. Was it their youth, their experiences in battle, their despair over what had happened to them and how society would react to them, or was it their excitement in coming together and sharing their dream, or a basic and total faith and trust in the American people? How did they imagine an organization such as they had formed could survive through the years without a belief that Americans cared?

They seemed to believe and trust that the financial support BVA would need would somehow materialize. In talking with some of the original blinded veteran founders of BVA, we get the very strong impression that the young men didn't want to ask for financial help. And for many, many years, our organization refused to make public appeals for the funds needed to push ahead with programs and services. It seems that the young men felt that, as blind people, it didn't look good for them to ask for financial help—it would appear as if they were just another group of blind folks appealing for money. It was a matter of understandable, perhaps commendable, pride, but it held BVA back for many years.

The subject of membership dues was hotly debated, with many of the original group feeling there should be no fees required at all to be a member of BVA. Finally, it was agreed that life membership in BVA would be five dollars. This would enable any and every blinded veteran to join and the nominal amount would still not impose a financial burden on a blinded veteran. Today our membership dues are somewhat higher, but still very nominal and still do not represent an income source for the Association.

The early days were rough indeed for BVA. We used donated office space, donated equipment and office furniture, and volunteer help. The American Foundation for the Blind was of tremendous assistance in the early years, collecting funds and making funds available to help the fledgling organization and to advance the work the blinded veterans were doing. It was more than money, too. Wonderful friends from the American Foundation for the Blind helped personally and advised and guided the young blinded veterans all along the way, and this long friendship has endured to this day.

In the early years, BVA was also fortunate to receive grants from the Women's Victory Bowling League. The League gave BVA three yearly grants of $25,000 to enable it to pay bills, continue printing the *BVA BULLETIN*, and to hire some part-time help. The money the League members had raised, by contributing a few cents per game, game by game, had added up to a lifesaver for BVA, and we will never forget.

This was the general situation BVA faced for many of these beginning years. Just when we would think we could go no further, friends would step forward to help. It has been really rough at times just keeping BVA afloat. One of our past administrative managers recalls having to borrow money to meet the small payroll BVA had at the time. But difficult times have made us more appreciative of the support we have been blessed to receive.

There also have been times when we have received some help from the federal government, although we receive no federal or state help at the present time. Following the end of the Vietnam war, the Department of Veterans Affairs gave BVA a contract to help reach and assist the many veterans blinded in the war. The Department of Labor also contracted with BVA to help them find jobs and job training opportunities for blinded Vietnam veterans.

However, the war in Vietnam is long over and the contracts and the money they provided have long since expired. But the work goes on. When the federal contracts expired, the BVA Board of Directors looked carefully at what had been done and the vast amount of work left to do, and voted to continue the BVA Field Service Program and fund it with whatever money we could raise. It was a courageous act, an act of faith, that the funds for this vital program would be there as BVA needed them.

We now raise all of our funds through direct mail appeals, and the money we raise through the appeals funds everything we do. It funds our Field Service Program, our *BVA BULLETIN,* our Scholarship Program, our direct assistance to blinded veterans attending blind rehabilitation programs, our legislative and public awareness programs—everything.

It's a difficult, time-consuming and expensive way to go about gathering funds. But it's the only way we have at the present time. We mail fund raising appeals to our many loyal friends seven times a year. It seems like a lot, but it takes that kind of effort if we are going to be able to continue helping blinded veterans.

Over the years, we have tried to mail quality appeal

letters to you: letters that show that BVA merits your support, and letters that demonstrate what we do with the money you send to us. As often as possible, we tell the stories of blinded veterans whom we have helped through your contributions. We also try to tell as much as we can about the problems and issues involved in blindness and how blinded veterans have managed to cope with blindness. We try to show you the good work we are doing and ask that you stand beside us as we try to do good work.

In all of our mail appeals we also try to give something back, to educate, to inspire, and let you know that you are more than someone we send letters to, that you are part of our BVA family.

Direct mail is an expensive way to raise money. Keeping costs down is a continuing challenge. Costs constantly creep up, making the direct mail program more expensive to conduct each year. The increasing cost of postage is one of the most worrisome; but everything, including the costs of paper, printing, and envelopes go up too. And we must pay a letter shop to assemble the letters and stuff the envelopes we send out.

We do the very best we can to keep costs down. We get the best competitive prices from suppliers and, by careful computer sorting, we are able to get the very best third class non-profit postage rates we can. Postal regulations have a great deal to do with the costs of a direct mail operation. Envelopes have to be a certain size and addresses have to be in certain places, and the whole package has to be within certain weight limits for postal machines to be able to process them.

Blinded veterans also are doing what they can to keep

BVA going. As time passed and some blinded veterans were able to finally get on their feet financially, they contributed what they could spare to help BVA. It has helped a lot. One good example, they raised the money for the down payment on our new National Headquarters building. For many years BVA conducted a building fund campaign among its members, and finally there was enough to purchase the building. Your support also helped immensely. Now we have a large plaque hanging in the lobby of our building and on it are the names of those who helped us in the campaign to raise funds for BVA's own home. So many of the names on the plaque are not those of blinded veterans but names of friends who helped us raise the money for our own building.

Major gifts from our friends have been especially important. Over the years, particularly in recent years, major gifts have been a primary factor in keeping the BVA Field Service Program operating. Just a few years ago, BVA was forced to reduce the number of Field Service Representatives and it looked like the Program might have to be drastically cut back. Fortunately, a major gift from a long time friend saved the day. But we are still concerned about the long range outlook for the Program. It's our most important activity and does the most for blinded veterans, but it's the most expensive too.

Recently, we were able to pay off the mortgage on our National Headquarters building. It was due in great part to a major gift, a bequest, from a friend whom we never knew we had. It was truly wonderful. There had been many months when we felt we had made a mistake in buying the building because the mortgage payments were so large and the money we were paying on the mortgage was mostly for interest payments, not helping anyone but the lender, certainly not blinded veterans. Thankfully, we are now past that problem, but those were terribly trying times.

Major gifts from our friends also helped us keep publishing the *BVA BULLETIN*. We have never missed an issue in the entire forty-eight years that we've been serving blinded veterans. We send the *BVA BULLETIN* out postage free, as free matter for the blind, but it costs a lot to have it printed. Gifts from our friends have enabled us to directly support blinded veterans attending VA Blind Rehabilitation Programs. Many of the veterans are too poor or ineligible for government help to pay their transportation to the rehabilitation centers, and many of them lack work clothes, shoes, socks and underwear. BVA pays for these whenever we are asked.

Our friends, through major gifts to BVA, have made it possible for us to purchase special reading and visual equipment that blinded veterans need to work. The technology many blinded veterans need is available but it is, unfortunately, very expensive. More needs to be done and we wish we could do more. Our Kathern Gruber Scholarship Program has been greatly helped by special gifts too. We provide scholarships to the spouses and children of needy blinded veterans. This is a costly program; We've all heard reports on the upward surge of college tuition; but the scholarships are important and we hope we can find the funds to increase the level of educational assistance we provide.

There are many other areas in which we hope we can find the funds to do more. The BVA Volunteer Service Program is a good example. Volunteers work without pay, but there are still expenses. Many of our volunteers travel over forty miles a day at their own expense to get to the office. It is not difficult to get a blinded veteran to volunteer; most will willingly extend themselves to help their fellow veterans, but it is difficult to say no when they ask for help in meeting their volunteer expenses. We need to equip our volunteer offices with computers and adaptive equipment so blinded veterans can do all they are able to do, but we don't have that kind of money now.

Many of our friends have called or written and commented on our direct mail fund raising program, suggesting that there may be other ways for BVA to raise the funds it needs now, and will need in the future. Every dollar means a great deal to us, and we feel we must continue with our proven method of fund raising. But major gifts from our friends are of such importance to BVA that we have initiated a new and special approach to fund raising we call our Planned Giving Program. We are trying to get the word to all of our BVA friends, our BVA family, that they can help build for the future by including BVA in their estate planning.

One part of our Planned Giving Program is our quarterly *FAMILY FORUM* newsletter which we are now sending to many of our friends. The *FAMILY FORUM* contains interesting articles on health and consumer issues, news of activities at BVA, and good information on estate planning and how one may be able to help BVA in the years to come through bequests and trusts and other forms of deferred giving. The effort is new to us and we are still learning. We have put together good information on estate planning that is easy to understand and should be of value to everybody when making plans for the future. And, if you are not yet receiving the *FAMILY FORM* and would like to be on our mailing list, please call us or drop us a note. You are part of our family too, and we know you will enjoy reading it.

"Do you mean that people gave money to help me when they don't know who I am? When they didn't even know my name?" The veteran had recently lost his sight and had called us to thank us after we bought him a round trip bus ticket to the Blind Rehabilitation Center. As we chatted, his words seemed to indicate that he thought we were just passing out money BVA had received from the government. We told him how it really was—that the money that got him to the place where he could learn to begin life anew had come from you, our friends. We told him it came to us a few dollars at a time. We told him that in many cases it came from Americans who were no better off than he. We told him it was from men and women, his fellow citizens, who still remembered and cared. Then he said, *"I didn't know. I didn't know that people cared that much about blinded veterans."*

And, dear friends, you have cared so much. We have kept faith and done our part, but you have made it all possible, and through your caring, the brave dream of those young blinded soldiers, the dream that began so long ago, will come true because you have shared the dream and stood with us through the years.

Afterword

We hope you enjoyed reading the stories and remembrances of blinded veterans and meeting the men and women of BVA, our National Officers, our volunteers, and our staff. We hope you have come to know and feel part of our BVA family, and feel part of the good work that is being done.

We have tried to share some of what we have experienced and learned as blinded veterans. We have tried to discuss blindness and its impact on the individual and the family from our own unique perspective, and hopefully have been able to dispel some of the mysteries and misconceptions about blindness.

Most of all, we've enjoyed sharing our own sense of accomplishment with you, the good news of how blinded veterans are being helped every day. It's a special pleasure to be able to share accomplishments with friends who care. We are proud of our nearly fifty year record of service to America's blinded veterans, and are determined to carry on our work until the battle is won. Blinded veterans cannot imagine what life would have been like if there had been no BVA. All of us, all blinded veterans, have been helped in many ways.

With faith in the future and trust in the good will of all Americans, we will carry on with our work until all blinded veterans have won their fight. On behalf of America's blinded veterans, we thank you.